Mysteries of

Mysteries of the Social Brain describes the scientific underpinnings of human behavior and values. Through the retelling of fascinating clinical stories of people with neurological conditions, this book explores the parts of the brain that allow humans to thrive as social and creative beings. The authors reveal the relevance of our brain circuits to our well-being—and the well-being of our societies—and show what happens when changes in our brain circuitry drive changes in empathy, altruism, moral beliefs, and creativity.

By integrating perspectives from neurology, psychology, psychiatry, and neuroscience, the stories in this book offer novel insights into the inner workings of the social brain and reveal groundbreaking findings from work in frontotemporal dementia, emotion, and the science of human values. This book showcases the novel discovery that creativity can emerge when there is decline in the brain's language systems, a finding that highlights the robust, yet underappreciated connections between science and art. Readers will learn about the biological basis of social behavior as well as simple steps that they can take to improve the functioning of their own social brains.

Miller and Sturm take us on an engaging dive into the field of behavioral neurology and neuroscience, exploring what we can learn from people with neurological conditions, and revealing the ways that neuroscience can change societies for the better. It will captivate general readers as well as clinicians and scientists who are interested in human social behavior, cognition, and emotion.

Bruce L. Miller, MD, is the A.W. and Mary Margaret Clausen Distinguished Professor of Neurology and Psychiatry and Behavioral Sciences at the University of California, San Francisco (UCSF), where he is the founding director of the UCSF Memory and Aging Center and Global Brain Health Institute. Dr. Miller studies social behavior and creativity in neurodegenerative disorders.

Virginia Sturm, PhD is the John Douglas French Alzheimer's Foundation Endowed Professor in the Departments of Neurology and Psychiatry and Behavioral Sciences at the University of California, San Francisco (UCSF). Dr. Sturm, an affective neuroscientist and neuropsychologist at the UCSF Memory and Aging Center, studies emotions, empathy, and social behavior in neurodegenerative disorders and neurodevelopmental conditions.

Like the best thrillers, *Mysteries of the Social Brain* is a true page-turner—taking us deep inside the tantalizing complexities of our remarkable brain and revealing how our neural circuitry makes us who we are. These are, yes, stories of great loss, but they also end up being testaments to the resiliency of the human spirit.

—**Josh Kornbluth**, *Monologuist & Filmmaker*

Mysteries of the Social Brain takes readers on an extraordinary journey into the complexities of human behavior and the brain. This book brilliantly illuminates how our brains shape empathy, fairness, creativity, and self-awareness. A masterful blend of science and storytelling, it offers deep insights into what makes us uniquely human. It is essential reading for anyone intrigued by the mysteries of the mind and the science behind our social nature.

—**Facundo Manes**, *MD, PhD, Neurologist, National Deputy of Argentina*

Mysteries of the Social Brain explores human behavior and creativity, comparing the functions of a healthy brain to one affected by disease. This understanding helps restore a sense of humanity to Dr. Miller's patients—a humanity often diminished by society due to their disease. This is something only Dr. Miller could achieve.

—**Emma Heming Willis**, *Frontotemporal Dementia Advocate*

Fascinating! Patient stories enhanced with clinical notes bring the importance of the social brain to light. The neuroscience of social behavior—described through circuitry, structures, and related experiences—spotlights the transformative role the social brain has on individuals as well as on caregivers, family, friends, and the global community. I want to cultivate these neural networks within my own brain! This book gave me the understanding and tools to do it.

—**Susan Schneider Williams**, *Artist and Advocate*

Mysteries of the Social Brain
Understanding Human Behavior Through Science

Bruce L. Miller and Virginia Sturm

Routledge
Taylor & Francis Group

NEW YORK AND LONDON

Designed cover image: © Caroline Prioleau

First published 2025
by Routledge
605 Third Avenue, New York, NY 10158

and by Routledge
4 Park Square, Milton Park, Abingdon, Oxon, OX14 4RN

Routledge is an imprint of the Taylor & Francis Group, an informa business

© 2025 Bruce L. Miller and Virginia Sturm

Library of Congress Cataloging-in-Publication Data
Names: Miller, Bruce L., 1949– author. | Sturm, Virginia, author.
Title: Mysteries of the social brain : understanding human behavior through
science / Bruce L. Miller and Virginia Sturm.
Description: Abingdon, Oxon ; New York, NY : Routledge, 2025. | Includes
bibliographical references and index. | Contents: Anatomy of the Social
Brain — Fairness — Empathy — Respect — Self-Awareness — Openness —
Creativity — Cultivating the Social Brain.
Identifiers: LCCN 2024042333 (print) | LCCN 2024042334 (ebook) | ISBN
9781032819846 (hardback) | ISBN 9781032814285 (paperback) | ISBN
9781003502357 (ebook)
Subjects: MESH: Social Behavior | Personality | Social Interaction | Neural
Pathways—physiology | Nervous System Diseases—psychology |
Neuropsychiatry—methods
Classification: LCC QP360 (print) | LCC QP360 (ebook) | NLM HM 1106 |
DDC 612.8—dc23/eng/20241231
LC record available at https://lccn.loc.gov/2024042333
LC ebook record available at https://lccn.loc.gov/2024042334

ISBN: 9781032819846 (hbk)
ISBN: 9781032814285 (pbk)
ISBN: 9781003502357 (ebk)

DOI: 10.4324/9781003502357

Typeset in Times New Roman
by codeMantra

This book is dedicated to Elliot Owen Clemens Miller, son of Bruce and Deborah Miller and brother of Hannah Whitehead Miller. Elliot was a beautiful and selfless man who lived the life of a bodhisattva. He died tragically in 2024. In his 40 years, Elliot touched the lives of many family members and friends, and he worked selflessly with the unhoused. Elliot was a philosopher and cook with a strong interest in religion, and he greatly influenced his father's thinking about meaning, courage, and the self.

Contents

We all count for one.

-Milton Miller

Prologue

"See one, do one, teach one" is a long-held mantra of medical training. But for most of us, seeing is harder than it seems. For behavioral neurologists, observing human behavior is an essential job requirement. One woman I met hugged the walls as she passed through her home's hallways, and another changed her style of dress and began to wear the clothes and makeup of a geisha. Still another collected dead animals from the side of the road and kept them, stiff with rigor mortis, in her living room. There was one man who killed ants one by one, tallying each death in a notebook, and another who believed there were creatures in his yard trying to kill him with a machete. Exploring the origins of these types of behavior is the focus of my life's work, and I have never been lacking things to do. The brain's mysteries are limitless.

I have always been interested in why humans act the way they do. In college, I was swept up by the cultural, musical, and political climate of the 1960s, and my experiences during this time sparked my interest in social behavior and creativity. Although I initially planned to teach high school, I changed course and studied chemistry, immersing myself in learning about molecules, medicine, and the brain. While in medical school in Vancouver, British Columbia, I had the opportunity to work in rural and urban environments and in different clinical settings—emergency rooms, intensive care units, psychiatry wards, and oncology clinics–but I was most drawn to the field of neurology. Ultimately, I chose to pursue behavioral neurology, a specialty within neurology that stands at the interface of philosophy and clinical care. Behavioral neurologists play very practical roles in diagnosing and treating neurological disorders and caring for patients and their families, but being a clinician and researcher in this field has also allowed me to explore the biology of human behavior. It is breathtaking to live and work within this duality.

During my behavioral neurology fellowship at the University of California, Los Angeles, I was fortunate to learn from neurologist Frank Benson, a true giant in the field. Dr. Benson was an exceptional clinician who translated complex principles of brain science into comprehensible bits. He started lessons with his observations about a patient's behavior, and he taught me to see and describe a clinical phenomenon before creating a theory to explain it.

DOI: 10.4324/9781003502357-1

"Most doctors don't really see patients," Dr. Benson said. "They fit patients into their preconceived theories, but they don't know how to observe." Dr. Benson, in contrast, stayed open to new ideas and described what he saw with extraordinary precision.

Although many other clinicians at the time (and still today) considered it unscientific to draw conclusions about the brain from a single patient, Dr. Benson emphasized that each person's story teaches us important lessons that are relevant to all of us. This was not a popular perspective among the other doctors. An attending physician once warned me that "the doctor with one case is a dangerous doctor." What he meant was that I should not put too much stock in things that I learned about the brain from any one person as these things probably did not reflect general truths. This bias against single cases still permeates neurology and psychiatry, but it is a point of view that I do not share. We cannot see how the brain functions with the naked eye, but we can learn about its operations through clinical observations. Of course, no single person is sufficient to unlock the brain's secrets, but great neuroscience frequently begins with a solitary clinical observation. There are endless mysteries about human behavior to investigate, and once we think we have solved some of them, new questions emerge. That is the ever-changing nature of science!

Another important principle that I learned from Dr. Benson and his colleague, Jeffrey Cummings, was that the left and right hemispheres of the brain have distinct functions. The left hemisphere has an affinity for words, grammar, reading, writing, mathematics, and logical thought, and the right hemisphere specializes in attention, visual processes such as painting, recognition of familiar faces, and social behavior. While at the time it was difficult to define its exact functions, we now know that the right hemisphere allows us to form relationships and to evaluate the intentions of others. Drs. Benson and Cummings were particularly interested in the anatomy of social behavior and solidified my passion for this area of study.

As a fellow, I had the opportunity to pursue my interests in this area when Dr. Benson introduced me to people with a neurodegenerative disorder called frontotemporal dementia, or FTD. Neurodegenerative disorders are progressive conditions that affect the brain, and FTD selectively injures the frontal and anterior temporal lobes. The manifestations of this illness fascinated me. While some patients exhibited profound changes in social behavior, others had disorders of language, and still others displayed enhanced visual creativity. Interactions with these patients and their families helped me to learn more about the parts of the brain (now we call them circuits) that are devoted to social behavior. Humans are wired to interact, connect, and innovate, but to this day, the biology of social behavior and creativity remain elusive. I began a quest to understand what we now call the "social brain" through my clinical interactions and research on FTD. Soon, I had assembled the largest cohort of people with FTD in the United States. Many of the stories in *Mysteries of the Social Brain* are about these individuals and their loved ones.

In 1998, I moved to the University of California, San Francisco (UCSF) where I started the Memory and Aging Center, a clinical and research center dedicated to the diagnosis, study, and treatment of neurodegenerative disorders. I have led the UCSF Memory and Aging Center for 25 years, and the incredible achievements of our team continue to astonish me. The dedication and imagination of our devoted staff members, students, fellows, researchers, and clinicians know no bounds. My colleagues at UCSF are bringing us closer to the day when there are treatments for neurodegenerative disorders including Alzheimer's disease and FTD, among others.

Throughout my career, I have mentored many talented trainees, and I try to pass Dr. Benson's lessons—and new ones—on to the next generation of scientists. One of these scientists is Virginia Sturm, Professor in the UCSF Departments of Neurology and Psychiatry and Behavioral Sciences, and my co-author of this book. I met Virginia when she started as a research coordinator at our center after graduating from Georgetown University. Soon after, she went on to pursue her PhD in clinical science (clinical psychology) at the University of California, Berkeley. In her doctoral work with Robert Levenson, she studied emotions and social behavior in neurodegenerative disorders. After graduate school, Virginia returned to the UCSF Memory and Aging Center and now directs the Clinical Affective Neuroscience Laboratory where she conducts pioneering studies of emotions in neurodegenerative disorders and neurodevelopmental conditions. While both hemispheres contribute to emotions and social behavior, much of our work has delineated the special importance of the right frontal and anterior temporal lobes in these domains.

In *Mysteries of the Social Brain*, we integrate lessons from neurology, neuroscience, psychiatry, and psychology to understand human behavior. Most of the chapters focus on people with neurodegenerative disorders (many with FTD) who exhibit profound changes in social behavior. In each chapter, from Chapters 2 to 7, we discuss a specific social ability—fairness, empathy, respect, self-awareness, openness, and creativity—and its underlying circuitry in the social brain. While some of the narratives may remind you of someone you know, others will seem less familiar. We changed the details in certain stories to protect the identities of the people we discuss while still capturing the true essence of their experiences. Although research about the social brain is beginning to address profound neuroscientific and philosophical questions, the stories of these individuals still have much to teach us about the exquisite complexity of the neural circuits that allow us all to thrive as social beings.

—Bruce L. Miller, MD

Introduction

In the ancient city of Çatalhöyük, nestled in the heart of modern-day Türkiye, families gathered for an evening feast as the sun dipped below the horizon. A young girl, adorned with colorful beads, paused to admire a large mural of a majestic red bull surrounded by a group of jubilant dancers. The mural, painted in rich ochre on a bright layer of white plaster, stretched across a wall of the community building, a central hub of activity in this bustling city. Nearby, a man played an upbeat melody on a flute made from the delicate bone of a bird, its notes mingling with the tantalizing aroma of a pig roasting over a stone pit. A group of women crushed seeds and legumes in intricately decorated ceramic bowls, preparing the meal they would soon share with their community. (Figure I.1)

Figure I.1 Replica of a mural found on a building wall in Çatalhöyük. Mural discovered by James Mellaart; original photograph by Arlette Mellaart. Used with permission by Alan Mellaart.

DOI: 10.4324/9781003502357-2

Ancient humans had social relationships much like ours. While *Homo sapiens* (Latin for "wise man") coexisted for a time with other types of early humans and hominins,[1] only *Homo sapiens* went on to populate the world. *Homo sapiens* may have had certain physical and cognitive advantages over their predecessors, such as the Neanderthals and Denisovans, but gains in physical prowess or intelligence alone cannot explain why *Homo sapiens* survived when these other groups did not. What then enabled these ancient humans to prosper as they did? The answer lies in their newfound social abilities.

Although often demoted to the realm of "soft skills," the ability to interact successfully with other people requires complex neural circuitry. Neuroscientist Leslie Brothers[2] and anthropologist Robin Dunbar[3] proposed that the brains of humans and great apes needed extra computational power to help them navigate their complex social environments. A system of connected structures in the brain, which we refer to as the "social brain," provided this additional power and allowed humans to communicate their ideas and to understand the perspectives of others. We now know that much of the human brain is devoted to our social relationships.

There is accumulating evidence that the human social brain has a broad array of essential responsibilities. By allowing us to discern the inner states of others and to feel their experiences, we are capable of empathy and deep emotional connections with others. We can cultivate self-awareness and treat others with fairness and respect. We use words, facial expressions, and gestures to express our thoughts and feelings, and we innovate through creative pursuits that come from the depths of our imaginations.

Despite a plethora of scientific advances, mysteries about the social brain abound. To gain clues about the social brain's organization, researchers can take various approaches. One way we can learn about the social brain is to compare the brains of humans with those of other species to see what makes the human brain unique. Studies of this kind suggest that *Homo sapiens* have larger volume and more densely packed neurons in the social brain than other species.[4] Researchers can also compare the human genome to those of other species to determine where there are differences in the genetic codes that set human brains apart.[5]

Another way to learn about the social brain is to take a close look at the lives of exceptional individuals. We can learn much from gifted individuals with noteworthy social skills. Sometimes, however, the most illuminating lessons come from people in whom the social brain no longer works as it once did. Their social behavior often deviates from the norm.

From birth, humans are attuned to other humans. Although social interest varies across people, for many individuals, nothing is more intriguing than other people. We develop close relationships with family members, friends, and colleagues and are interested in the details of their lives. We are even curious about people we do not know. Neighbors peer from behind curtains to see who is walking down the sidewalk, café patrons eavesdrop on mundane conversations of strangers to hear details of their everyday experiences, and fans follow celebrities online to share the thrills of their various successes and scandals. We seek out interactions with others, and it is painful when we are isolated from or rejected by others. Many of us spend an inordinate amount of time thinking about other people's opinions and lives, and we ruminate about how they feel about us. We replay our conversations to ensure effective communication and worry about how to express our thoughts and feelings in considerate yet honest ways. Why do we put in so much effort? Because our lives depend on social relationships.

Before *Homo sapiens* settled in cities like Çatalhöyük over 9,000 years ago,[6] they lived a more solitary existence. Wandering from place to place in small hunter-gatherer tribes, they foraged for plants and berries and hunted animals in ever-changing settings and conditions. As their social and cognitive abilities developed, they wandered less and began to put down roots. At first, they formed small villages, but bustling cities with thousands of residents soon followed. It was in these early communities that ancient humans used and refined the social brain systems that we explore in this book. These people, our ancestors, no longer saw themselves as passive benefactors of nature's offerings, but they began to view themselves as active agents who could influence the resources their environment produced.[7] Increased proximity gave them more opportunities to spend time together.[8] Through frequent social interactions, they formed enduring relationships and collaborated on larger projects. Even small settlements soon grew rapidly with advances in areas such as farming and animal domestication.

Like humans today, ancient humans needed to be good at many things to manage their social environments. Whereas people in hunter-gatherer societies were free to leave and join a more welcoming group when there was a disagreement, it was critical for members of stable communities to reconcile after challenges. Loyal connections were essential in times of strife, and ancient humans relied on others for physical as well as emotional support. To form lasting friendships, they needed empathy and self-awareness. The ability to understand oneself and others would have helped them to work together and to strategize about how to manage their community's needs.

Cohabiting in close-knit groups provided ancient humans with numerous advantages. With greater resources, the people in these communities could better protect the vulnerable and care for the sick and injured. In times of scarcity, group living also provided residents with greater economic security by ensuring food and shelter. As problems inevitably arose when resources were unevenly divided, people began to look to leaders to resolve inequities.[9] There was likely an increasing appreciation for fairness and a deepening respect for social rules and order. Festive gatherings were frequent in these communities and promoted conflict resolution and goodwill.

With a more complex social brain, *Homo sapiens* worked together and achieved things that their predecessors could not. Their abundant social interactions ignited openness and creativity, and the arts proliferated. By offering people new ways to destress from the pressures of group living and to convey their ideas, the arts allowed them to commemorate shared beliefs and traditions.[10] According to psychologist Michael Tomasello, these new forms of expression not only promoted better communication between individuals and groups but also deepened their social bonds.[11] They learned from each other and created cultures built on cooperation that benefitted them and their societies.[12] Through growing artistic practices, ancient humans honored their communal experiences and passed their knowledge on to generations to come.

At first, their art was simple. *Homo sapiens* began to decorate their bodies by wearing beads and coloring their skin with dyes and paints.[13] The colors and designs that they used in their jewelry and bodily decorations often had social significance, signaling family connections and allegiances within the community. As ancient humans developed as visual artists, their creations moved beyond the body. They pierced shells and engraved ochre slabs with geometric patterns that they may have seen in nature. The physical shapes and uneven surfaces of natural objects may also have motivated their earliest stone tools, which bore a strong resemblance to the rocks from which they originated.

Soon, the inspirations for their creations began to emerge from their imaginations. Unlike their predecessors, whose more isolated lifestyle offered few reasons for them to share their experiences, ancient humans began to turn their internal mental worlds into external representations that others could behold. They visualized and created artwork and tools that did not yet exist and made mental roadmaps to produce their pieces one step at a time.[14] This ability to detach from the here and now and to generate possibilities for an unexperienced future lies at the heart of human creativity and led to rapid innovations in tools as well as art.

Ancient humans did not merely dabble in the arts but put enormous time and effort into their handiwork and exhibited incredible technical skills.[15] When they started to use symbols to express themselves, their art became even more elaborate. They painted animals with special significance on rocks and in caves. They crafted music and carved instruments from the smooth ivory of woolly mammoths and the hollow bones of birds. They etched repeating motifs with symbolic meanings on ceramics and textiles, and they created jewelry with colors and designs that distinguished among social groups. Through their artwork, ancient humans communicated important information about social rules and values.

During this period, ancient humans also developed spoken language. Each word is a unique combination of sounds that refers to an object, living creature, mental state, action, or any other concept that the human mind can create. Words themselves are social in that, to be effective communication tools, people must have a shared knowledge of their meanings. Learning to speak and understand language is inherently social as we acquire the meanings of words and the rules of grammar by hearing and imitating other people. By stringing words together, we can create an infinite array of sentences to express an endless number of ideas.[16] Like images and sounds, words are the building blocks of creativity.

Although the first texts did not appear until later, approximately 5,500 years ago, the precursors of written language were evident much earlier. It was long a mystery why ancient humans clustered their cave paintings on certain surfaces deep in chambers that were hard to access, but recent studies have revealed that the locations of these paintings were deliberate. By placing paintings of hoofed animals in areas of the caves that generated echoes akin to the sound of herds of running animals and paintings of cats in quieter areas with less pronounced reverberations, these ancient artists incorporated the acoustic properties of the caves into their drawings and forged associations between auditory and visual information.[17] This was where humans first linked sounds to pictures and, eventually, sounds to letters and words. These early paintings were not only compelling visual art but also laid the foundations for written language. (Figure I.2)

The social and creative abilities of *Homo sapiens* flourished when they began to live together in communities, and by working together, they achieved things that other species could not. Their technical innovations and social connections led to improvements in physical health, and their civilizations thrived as they became better friends and neighbors.

Figure I.2 Cave paintings were placed in areas that reflected the acoustic properties of the cave chambers.

1 Anatomy of the Social Brain

Humans have a social brain like no other. By supporting emotions, language, and creativity, the social brain allows us to do the many things that we need to survive. To guide your understanding of the complexities of the social brain, we begin by reviewing five principles that provide background information and a scientific framework for the chapters that follow. These principles not only apply to the people in this book but also pertain to all of us.

The Social Brain Engages Multiple Neural Networks

When it comes to the brain's structural architecture, all brains have a similar layout. The human brain has two hemispheres, and a deep fissure at the brain's midline divides the left hemisphere from the right. Each hemisphere has different capabilities, but there is significant crosstalk across the brain.[18] The left hemisphere is important for verbal and symbolic abilities including speech, language, and mathematics. The right hemisphere, in contrast, is critical for nonverbal abilities such as social behavior, emotions, empathy, and visual processes. Both hemispheres work together to help humans to communicate and to coexist as social beings.

In humans, much of the brain is composed of the cerebral cortex—the thick, outer layers of tissue on the surface of the brain. The surface of the cerebral cortex has many folds and wrinkles. Those folds and wrinkles expand the brain's surface area so that it can engage more neurons in each function. The cerebral cortex can be divided into the frontal, temporal, parietal, and occipital lobes. The frontal and temporal lobes are in the anterior (front) of the brain, and the parietal and occipital lobes are in the posterior (back) part. These structures are important for the senses as well as many other critical cognitive and emotional abilities such as memory, reasoning, language, analytical thinking, personality, decision-making, and learning. Beneath the cerebral cortex lie numerous subcortical structures that are important for many involuntary bodily functions such as regulation of breathing and temperature.

DOI: 10.4324/9781003502357-3

As we shall see, numerous cortical and subcortical structures are essential for social behavior (Figure 1.1).

The human brain is built of 86 billion neurons. These neurons are organized into networks (or circuits)[19] that create strong connections across the brain and allow various structures to work together. To help you picture how these networks operate, imagine for a moment that the brain is like a city. Cities, like brains, have certain basic components. While brains have different lobes and structures, cities have grocery stores, schools, gas stations, hospitals, et cetera. Both brains and cities are more than the sum of their parts, however, and need connections between various areas to function properly. Like roads linking remote areas of the city, networks connect neurons in even distant parts of the brain and allow them to work together. When one neuron in a network fires, the others fire, and when one neuron in a network is silent, the others follow suit. This type of synchronized activity across neurons allows each network to perform its own distinct functions. Certain networks activate when we perform tasks. Some networks allow us to move our limbs with precision, and others enable us to solve math problems or read the newspaper. Other networks spring into action when we are at rest and enable us to daydream. These are the networks that also allow us to reminisce or ruminate about our previous words and actions. In the social brain, multiple networks

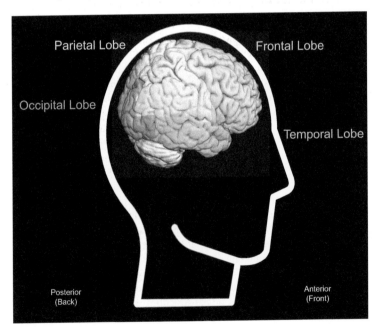

Figure 1.1 The lobes of the human brain.

associated with subtle alterations in brain structure and function that make some activities harder than they once were. Just as there is normal wear and tear in any city over time—roads need repaving, trees need trimming, and buildings need a fresh coat of paint—our brains also change as we age and may become less efficient in some areas. Older adults tend to perform cognitive tasks less quickly than younger people, and motor speed and other physical abilities often decline. For most, remembering people's names and finding words becomes more challenging in the later years of life. Still, mild difficulties in these areas are not usually a cause for concern.

Advancing age may render the brain networks that support cognition and movement slower or less efficient, but social brain circuits continue to function even in the later decades of life. Some older adults experience chronic negative emotions as they age because they do not have the social support that they need. Psychiatrist Brian Lawlor notes that loneliness, an epidemic in later life, is detrimental to many areas of their functioning. Lonelier people have worse sleep, blood pressure, immune function, cognition, and mood than those who feel less isolated.[25] Compared to older adults with an active lifestyle and rich social network, those with fewer social ties are at higher risk for cognitive and physical decline. Our bodies have close connections with our social brains, and relationships are essential for our survival. Without ongoing cognitive stimulation and social engagement, our mental and physical health suffer.

The good news is that we can use our social brains to help us flourish as we age. Many older adults experience greater well-being than their younger counterparts and describe their later years as the happiest time of their lives.[26] Positive emotions counteract the effects of negative emotions and have restorative influences on the mind and body.[27] By focusing more on positive information than they did in the past, older adults can better savor pleasant experiences and cherish life's meaningful moments.[28] Whereas younger adults prioritize expanding their social connections and spending time with new people, psychologist Laura Carstensen has found older adults devote more of their energy to maintaining relationships with a smaller circle of close friends and family.[29] As we age, we become better at putting life's challenges into perspective. We are also more adept at filling our lives with joy and purpose and cultivating deep social connections. In the later years of life, people can use their social and emotional skills to strengthen their interpersonal bonds and to make a positive impact on their friends, children, grandchildren, and extended family.

Alterations in Behavior Reveal the Organization of the Social Brain

In a city, we never appreciate how well something works until it no longer functions well. We might not realize how smoothly traffic flows until streets are closed for repairs, and we might not be grateful for an efficient subway system until it shuts down. We tend to take our own health for granted in a comparable way. We may not pay attention to the fine movements of our hands until we break a wrist, or we may overlook the unwavering beat of our heart until we sense an irregular rhythm. We may also be shortsighted when it comes to appreciating our brains and minds, overlooking our wondrous social and cognitive abilities until something goes awry.

Unfortunately, problems with our physical health become more likely as we get older. Although many adults prosper in their later years, others do not fare as well. Advancing age often brings various ailments including diseases that affect the brain. Neurodegenerative disorders are progressive illnesses that change the way brain networks function. People with neurodegenerative disorders exhibit gradual decline in thinking, movement, and behavior. When a neurodegenerative disorder begins, specific proteins in the brain misfold and aggregate in clumps, altering how neurons function. These neurons lose their connections with other neurons and eventually die, causing the brain tissue to shrink (or atrophy).

There are many different types of neurodegenerative disorders, and each of them manifests as a specific set of symptoms and signs. Symptoms are changes that people themselves notice, and signs are manifestations of a disease that clinicians perceive in them. Alzheimer's disease is the most common neurodegenerative disorder and the most well-known. While people with Alzheimer's disease often have difficulty recalling recent memories (such as what they ate for dinner yesterday or who came to visit the previous weekend), some have trouble finding their way around familiar places, making plans, and finding the words they want to say. Other neurodegenerative disorders disrupt different brain regions and cause distinct changes. In frontotemporal dementia, or FTD, people lose their ability to maintain relationships and to communicate with others. There are many other neurodegenerative disorders including Parkinson's disease, Lou Gehrig's disease (also known as amyotrophic lateral sclerosis or ALS), dementia with Lewy bodies, and others—each with their own constellation of symptoms and signs.

The nature of the early symptoms and signs offers clues about which disorder a person has. At first, the changes in the brain are mild and selective. Just as cities may have different problems—one may have a library with a leaky roof and a dilapidated stairwell, and another may have a baseball stadium that is in disrepair—people with neurodegenerative disorders have different symptoms that reflect alterations in specific brain regions.

As neurodegenerative disorders progress slowly over years, even decades, the disease spreads to other brain regions and symptoms gradually worsen. If many structures in a city deteriorate, the city will struggle. The same is true of our brains. Eventually, people with neurodegenerative disorders lose the ability to perform daily tasks and care for themselves. When they cross this threshold, we call their condition "dementia." Dementia is often caused by a neurodegenerative disorder but can be due to other reasons such as a stroke, tumor, or metabolic deficiency such as a thyroid problem or low vitamin B12 (Figure 1.3).

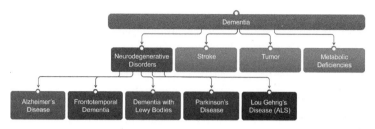

Figure 1.3 Neurodegenerative disorders are characterized by unique sets of changes in behavior, cognition, and movement.

Obtaining a correct diagnosis for someone with a neurodegenerative disorder is important because it points to the underlying protein, or proteins, responsible for their symptoms. Treatments that stop neurodegenerative disorders in their tracks or recover an individual's lost abilities are yet to be discovered, but research in this area is moving rapidly. Medicines that slow cognitive decline in Alzheimer's disease have recently become available. Now, more than ever, there is hope that new therapies, and even cures, are on the horizon. As protein-specific medicines become available, an accurate diagnosis will be critical.

Weakness in One Part of the Social Brain Can Promote Strengths in Other Parts of the Brain

Over time, problems in one part of a city may have more widespread effects on the surrounding neighborhoods. If the movie theater is closed for renovations, fewer people will take the subway line in that direction or wander the sidewalks in its vicinity. The shops and restaurants around the movie theater may lose business as that part of the city becomes less popular and vibrant. In the early stages of neurodegenerative disorders, there may also be selective dysfunction in specific regions of the brain. Diminished functioning in these brain areas can cause devastating losses for individuals as well as their families. Sometimes, however, problems in one part of the brain can also lead to unexpected changes in other areas.

Just as the movie theater, modern art museum, and pickleball courts compete for patrons, certain brain networks are also in competition. Neurons in the same network fire in tandem, but the synchronous activity of one network's neurons may inhibit the activity of neurons in another network. That is, when activity in one network is high, activity in the other is low. We can toggle between different states and adjust to new situations by activating and deactivating competing circuits. As we experience different feelings or move our bodies in various ways, brain networks engage and disengage in a fluid manner. This type of neural flexibility allows us to perform a wide range of activities. A problem in one of these networks, however, can affect others. When the movie theater is closed in a city, its regular patrons may go other places to try new things. Without competition from the movie theater, more people may head to the modern art museum or the pickleball courts. The modern art museum and pickleball courts, in turn, may see crowds like never before.

A similar thing can happen in the brain—when certain circuits close for business, others may shift into overdrive. Neuropsychologist Narinder Kapur noted that, in humans and other animals, damage in one brain region can have a surprising effect. Damage in one region can improve the functioning of another region.[30] After having a tumor and the surrounding brain tissue removed, people who once stuttered spoke more fluently. Cats with brain lesions that left them without vision responded more quickly to auditory cues than cats who could see. In some cases, these newfound abilities even surpassed the performance of people and animals without a brain injury. How is that possible?

In the brain, damage to a region that usually acts as a brake can "release" (or accentuate) a circuit that was once inhibited. A stroke, tumor, or head injury can free this repressed circuit from its normal shackles and allow it to blossom. A comparable type of release can also occur in neurodegenerative disorders and increase activity in specific brain networks. In these cases, people may develop new strengths and talents, even in the setting of dementia and other losses.

Social Brain Function Varies across People

Each of us has a social brain, but social savviness varies enormously across people. There are normal differences in all our abilities—some of us are born great spellers but poor tennis players, and others are standouts in graphic design but not math. Our social skills are no different.

Variation in our social brain wiring influences how we respond in different situations. People can react in many ways to the same social information, and we can begin to understand their behavior by considering how their social brains function. To appreciate how circuits in the social brain operate, let us take an everyday example. Imagine you are at the grocery store, and you see an older woman—we will call her Sophia—slip and fall in a puddle of water. With her bag of groceries in hand, she lands on the floor and cries out in alarm as her groceries scatter throughout the aisle. If we could replay this scene in slow motion, we could gain clues about what happened in your social brain, and in the social brains of Sophia and those around her, as this situation unfolded.

Let us say there were a few other shoppers nearby who also witnessed the accident, and you notice that each had a different reaction to Sophia's plight. First, you see a man in an olive-green jacket to your right who touches his

Figure 1.4 There is variability in how different people react in the same social situation. Illustration by Brittany Morin.

face with his hand. You can see his lips stretched and parted underneath his hand and his eyebrows raised and knitted together. He quickly averts his eyes and turns to rummage through the produce section. You next glance to your left where you see a woman with orange pants roll her eyes and purse her lips together. She walks right past Sophia without a second look. A woman in a gray sweater then approaches Sophia and crouches down to ask how she is doing. With furrowed eyebrows, this woman asks a man nearby to find an employee for assistance (Figure 1.4).

As each of these individuals takes in the situation, multiple brain regions spring into action. First, sensory information about the scene enters the brain. The occipital lobes allow the onlookers to see what happened, and the parietal lobes enable them to sense their own position in the environment and to perceive the spatial relationships between the other people and objects around them. While accurate perceptual information is important for understanding the physical details of the situation, systems in the social brain are critical for influencing what happens next. On the lateral surface of the temporal lobes, the posterior regions of the superior temporal gyrus process the bodily movements and the voices of the other people. These areas allow the onlookers to understand the meaning of Sophia's crumpled posture on the floor and the significance of her whimpers. The fusiform gyrus, an area that lies at the bottom of the temporal lobes, is specialized for perceiving faces. This this region helps them to examine Sophia's facial features and to determine whether they recognize her.

The anterior temporal lobes, areas that cap each temporal lobe, store information about objects, people, and emotions. Using semantic knowledge stored in the anterior temporal lobes, the onlookers can recognize that Sophia's red face and glistening eyes are signs of embarrassment and pain. The anterior temporal lobes have tight connections with the amygdala, a structure within the medial temporal lobes that detects and responds to important cues in the environment. With the anterior cingulate cortex, which lies at the brain's midline in the frontal lobes, the amygdala generates changes in the body during emotions. Both structures likely activated in Sophia and in the onlookers who watched her fall. The anterior insula, a region buried between the frontal and temporal lobes, receives continuous streams of information about the internal conditions of the body and is critical for experiences of emotions and empathy. Activity in the anterior insula helped the onlookers to become aware of their own feelings.

In this situation, each person experienced a different emotion because each had a distinct impression of what happened. While the man in the green jacket and the woman in the gray sweater shared Sophia's feelings of embarrassment and pain, the woman with the orange pants displayed contempt and irritation. We cannot know for sure why she had this reaction, but it is possible that she used other information to come to a different conclusion about the situation. Perhaps she thought Sophia was faking her injuries, or perhaps she had seen Sophia perform what she assumed to be similar theatrics before. Or, worse yet, perhaps the woman in the orange pants did not respect older people and used her preconceived notions to override any feelings of empathy. Another possibility is that the woman in the orange pants was just not very attuned to social information and did not notice that Sophia was in significant pain. This impression, too, would have led her to be annoyed that Sophia had interfered with her shopping trip.

The emotions that the onlookers experienced influenced their actions.[31] While the woman with the orange pants felt little empathy and walked past Sophia without guilt or remorse, the man in the green jacket and the woman in the gray sweater both shared Sophia's distress. What each of these onlookers did next to manage their feelings, however, was not the same and may have reflected activity in other brain regions.

Perhaps Sophia's situation was too personal for the man in the green jacket because he, too, had a recent fall. Or perhaps his social brain had always been highly sensitive to the pain of others. Either way, the man in the green jacket was overwhelmed by his own negative feelings. By engaging the dorsolateral prefrontal cortex, an area on the sides of the frontal lobes near the top of the brain, he was able to distract himself from his discomfort by looking through the produce section. While this strategy helped to ease his nerves, it did not help Sophia.

The woman in the gray sweater, in contrast, helped Sophia and felt good doing so. To manage her own feelings of unease, she activated the lateral orbitofrontal cortex, an area of the frontal lobes that lies above the eyes at the sides of the brain. The medial orbitofrontal cortex, the part of the orbitofrontal cortex at the brain's midline, may also have helped her to see the potential upsides of assisting. She may have realized that helping Sophia would make them both feel better. The medial orbitofrontal cortex, along with adjacent regions in the medial prefrontal cortex, motivated the woman in the gray sweater to approach Sophia despite her initial anxiety.

And all of this would have happened in a matter of seconds! The social brain is critical for many interpersonal skills, and variation in behavior reflects differences in social brain wiring or activity. In some cases, the outliers in social behavior offer unique insights into the neural underpinnings of our most human abilities including fairness, empathy, respect, self-awareness, openness, and creativity. With these five principles in mind, we are ready to delve into the stories of people who have changes in these core components of human behavior. These are the real stories that we turn to next.

2 Fairness

One of the most complex and mysterious human values is fairness. By fostering trust and goodwill, fairness is critical for the creation and maintenance of successful societies.[32] In humans and many other species, the quest for fairness is deeply ingrained in the circuitry of the brain and helps individuals to cooperate in large groups. Even guppies take turns leading their schools into dangerous waters, swimming back and forth to share the risk of confronting predators.[33] Rats share chocolate with other rats for no apparent reason other than just being nice,[34] and capuchin monkeys give grapes to their comrades who have none.[35] By motivating humans and other animals to share resources, a sense of fairness encourages each member of a species to give others their due.

Humans have an acute sense of fairness, but we quickly learn that life, unfortunately, is not always fair. At an early age, children realize when their siblings, friends, or peers receive more praise or rewards than they deserve.[36] In adulthood, our everyday lives are full of instances that violate our sense of fairness—a moviegoer jumps ahead of others in line, a little league coach plays their own child more than other talented teammates, and an inexperienced job applicant with connections to the boss gets hired instead of a seasoned professional. Our brains are wired to perceive unfairness, and each of these injustices, however small, evokes a reaction that motivates us to rectify the situation.[37] This complex and wondrous value has been a critical component of human history, and without a sense of fairness, the world would be a different place. Indeed, we might never have survived as a species without this trait.

There may be certain aspects of each of our lives that seem unfair. None of us has control over the time and place in which we are born or the families and circumstances in which we grow up. And we have no sway over the DNA that we inherit from our parents. Our genes and experiences work together to shape our social brains over the course of our lives. Sometimes, we are lucky, and supportive relationships and societal adaptations offset inequities that we face. Other times, our experiences can make it harder for us to perceive what is fair and to make things right when someone is treated unjustly. Such was the case of Jaime, whose story illustrates how genes and experiences interact to instill a sense of fairness in the social brain.

DOI: 10.4324/9781003502357-4

Dr. Miller's Clinical Note

I met Jaime and her husband, Curt, on a dreary November morning. Jaime leaned to the left in her small wheelchair as Curt pushed her up the ramp to the building where my office was located. Jaime's short gray hair framed an emotionless face. Curt, a lean and broad-shouldered man, had dressed her in a velour pink tracksuit and covered her in blankets. As he wheeled Jaime into my office, she stared at me with an ice-cold glare that made me feel as if she were studying me with contempt.

Jaime was extremely sick by the time I first met her. She was only 56 years old, but from my first look at her frail body I knew she had been ill for some time. I assembled a list of questions that I needed to ask to determine what was wrong and whether Jaime had a neurodegenerative disorder. It was hard to imagine the powerful woman that Curt would describe in the woman who sat before me, but I had learned to expect the unexpected.

Neurodegenerative disorders are usually slow, creeping through the brain and causing gradual changes in a person's thinking, movement, and behavior. When a person with one of these conditions has had symptoms for a long time, it can be difficult to disentangle problems that appeared earlier from those that came later. Like a good detective, a clinician must delve deep into a person's life history to understand their baseline personality and abilities and then assess the extent to which they have changed from the person that they once were. It is important to uncover the first symptoms because they offer clues about where in the brain the problems began and which disease the person has. By conducting detailed neurological, psychiatric, and neuropsychological examinations in addition to a life history, a clinician gathers information that sheds light on the parts of a person's brain that are working well and those that are struggling.

"Can you please help Jaime onto the table?" I asked Curt. Jaime grimaced as Curt lifted her out of the wheelchair. She flared her nostrils and pressed her lips, facial movements that usually signify anger. Jaime's expression was disquieting, but given her weakened condition, I withheld judgment as to her true feelings. In some neurological disorders, there can be a mismatch between the facial expressions that people display and the experiences that they feel. People with Parkinson's disease, for example, may have limited facial expressivity that masks feelings of happiness or sadness, while those with Lou Gehrig's disease (or ALS) sometimes exhibit uncontrollable bursts of laughter despite experiencing severe depression. It was hard to know how Jaime really felt inside.

Once Jaime was sitting comfortably on the table, I conducted a brief neurological examination. At first, I was not sure how much of what I said Jaime understood, but I sensed that she comprehended more than was apparent from the silence that filled the room after each of my questions. I raised my hands in front of her, and she blinked when I wiggled the fingers of my right hand, and then my left. Her response was normal, which told me that she could see movement with both eyes. Next, I assessed whether Jaime could track movements. I walked back and forth in front of her and noted that her eyes followed me as I crossed the room—a good sign that suggested that the eye movement systems in the frontal and parietal lobes and brainstem all worked well.

I looked closely at Jaime's body to determine whether there were problems with her muscles or motor functioning. Her face was immobile, but the left half of her mouth drooped slightly, making her mouth appear sad on that side. The muscles in Jaime's left arm and leg were weak, but her right side was stronger, almost normal. I pulled a short metal rod from my bag and scratched the bottoms of her feet, a test of the Babinski reflex. Her toes spread apart, and her big toes curled upward. Although this reaction is typical in infants, in adults it is a sign that parts of the motor system are failing.

Upon completing my examination, I asked Curt if he could put Jaime back in her wheelchair. He moved cautiously and was careful to avoid making sudden movements around her. As Curt reached down to lift Jaime off the table, she lunged out and grabbed his neck with her right hand, the side of her body that was still strong. Her tight grip blocked his windpipe, and the sudden fear in Curt's eyes told me he was having trouble breathing. Startled by Jaime's strength, I jumped toward the table. With Curt's help, I pried Jaime's hand off his throat. Curt doubled over in a coughing fit, his face beet red. He was exhausted.

Few moments in my medical career have unsettled me more. Here was a man who devoted all his resources to protecting and caring for Jaime, and she had just violently attacked him. "Are you alright?" I asked Curt quietly. Curt nodded, blushing in embarrassment. He moved a few steps away from me and Jaime, looked out the window, and took a deep breath. It was several minutes before he was ready to speak again and to tell me Jaime's story.

Jaime grew up in a small town in the Midwest. When she was two weeks old, Jaime's father abandoned her and her mother, Martha. In Jaime's first years of life, Martha struggled to make ends meet, but when Jaime turned four, Martha began a business that created and sold board games. After a successful marketing campaign, one of Martha's games, *"Heroes and Villains,"* became wildly popular and made her the wealthiest woman in town. While Martha's success was due, in part, to her hard work and ingenuity, she was also ruthless in her business ventures. Martha was willing to take risks in her investments when others shied away, and this unorthodox strategy worked well for her bottom line. She lacked concern for others, and while her callous interpersonal style did not make her many friends, it did help make her rich.

Martha was generous to Jaime with material items but was less giving when it came to her affection. She bought every toy, dollhouse, and fancy dress that Jaime desired but was otherwise distant, providing Jaime with little attention or warmth. Absorbed with her business and a rotating cast of boyfriends, Martha often disappeared for weeks at a time, either working overtime for endless hours or taking vacations with new lovers. Apart from her peers at school and Martha's short-lived romantic interests, Jaime had little contact with people. She longed for siblings, cousins, or friends to play with but often spent time alone.

Martha's frequent absences upset Jaime when she was young, but as a teenager she began to appreciate her mother's laissez-faire parenting. By Jaime's first year of high school, she had established a reputation for hosting the most raucous parties in town. Jaime drew people to her as she was both smart and alluring. She had a delicate face, blonde hair, blue eyes, and a flair for fashion. Despite her popularity, Jaime was cliquish and aloof and, like her mother, made few lasting friends. When Jaime was 17, she became pregnant. Martha sent her away to live in a special girls' home where Jaime gave birth to a baby boy whom she gave up for adoption. Jaime never returned to her hometown again.

After finishing high school at a private boarding school, Jaime obtained bachelor's degrees in engineering and business, an unusual combination and remarkable achievement for a woman growing up in the 1950s. After college, she started a successful sports consulting company and designed novel exercise programs that were valuable for college athletic teams. Jaime had an intuitive ability with computers, which she used in her company years before they became a routine part of the workplace. Like Martha, Jaime was determined, strategic, and uncompromising when it came to business. She used her charm to lure people into negotiations and had no hesitation in exploiting their weaknesses. Jaime soon proved herself to be a shrewd entrepreneur. Her personal life, however, was a different story. She had a series of brief relationships including three short marriages—the first two ended in acrimonious divorces, and the third she annulled after only six days. Jaime had no enduring partners. Until Curt.

Jaime first met Curt during her sophomore year of high school. Curt, then a senior, was attractive but shy and lacking in confidence. Intimidated by

Jaime's beauty and wealth, Curt idolized her from afar. Curt worked through high school to help his family pay the bills. After graduation, he entered the Naval Academy and spent time in Vietnam. Curt became an accomplished officer and received a silver star for his bravery in battle, and he left the military in his mid-forties. As a young adult, Curt dated a few women, one for a decade, but never married. Although he lost touch with Jaime after high school, Curt increasingly thought about her over the years. Eventually, he decided to find her.

Jaime and Curt reconnected when she was in her late forties and Curt, his early fifties. Soon they were married—a dream that Curt had harbored as a teenager finally came true. At first, their vastly different personalities worked well together. Curt was glad to manage the household responsibilities such as the cooking and shopping, activities for which he had his own efficient systems. Jaime was never overly concerned with managing the fine details of her finances, so banking and bill paying also fell to Curt. Although Jaime had failed to pay her taxes the previous year, Curt smoothed things over and arranged a settlement with the government.

Curt noticed changes in Jaime's social behavior not long after they married. Although Jaime had always been aloof and never particularly generous, she began to treat people who worked in shops, restaurants, and hotels with outright contempt. She became more dismissive of Curt's friends and family and, after one year of marriage, told him that she wanted nothing to do with them. Curt maintained these relationships but kept Jaime unaware that he still had contact. For their second wedding anniversary, Curt and Jaime vacationed in the Caribbean. Soon after arriving, Jaime announced that she would be spending the remainder of the trip with a man she had just met in the bar. She left Curt alone in the hotel for the entire week and reappeared the night before they were to return home. Devastated but still in love, Curt remained committed to Jaime, but her infidelity marked the beginning of a downhill slide for their relationship, and for Jaime herself.

Over time, Jaime's actions became more troubling. She argued with Curt about most things—from her extravagant spending on personal items to her snide comments to strangers and acquaintances. Her actions bewildered Curt, but he tended to blame himself, or Martha, for Jaime's worsening behavior. Jaime's cruelty and coldness only became more extreme, and on one occasion at a restaurant, she berated Curt in public and dumped a plate of hot food onto his lap. In addition to her increasing outbursts, Jaime became overly familiar with strangers, openly discussing everything from her political opinions to intimate details of her sexual relationships. In a cloying voice, she would say to men she had just met, "You are cute, sir," eerily mimicking Curt's military formality and embarrassing both him and the stranger.

As Jaime got older, she experienced few emotions other than anger. Emotions often arise without much warning and change our thoughts, feelings, and actions. During moments of anger, our heart rate and breathing quicken.

Our face may flush, and there may be alterations in our voice, posture, and facial expression. The kinds of changes that occur in our organs and muscles during anger (and other emotions) are similar in all of us and can help us to understand how others feel.[38] While not all emotions are pleasant to experience, each serves an important function in our lives. Negative emotions alert us to danger, contamination, loss, and injustice, and positive emotions help us to connect with others.[39] Anger differs from other negative emotions in more ways than one. Although negative emotions such as fear, sadness, disgust, and embarrassment prompt us to withdraw, anger encourages us to approach and to take actions that make matters right. Anger also relies on brain systems in the left hemisphere more than in the right.[40]

Curt had experienced more than his fair share of injustices, but if he ever felt angry at Jaime, he rarely showed it. If anything, Jaime's worsening treatment of others, including him, inspired him to become more caring. Curt channeled even his most negative experiences with Jaime into gestures of compassion and generosity rather than acts of bitterness and rage. He even went beyond what most would consider fair in his treatment of Jaime. Curt exhibited remarkable altruism despite suffering at the hands of an illness that mercilessly robbed him of his relationship with the woman he loved.

As I listened to Curt's story, it was almost incomprehensible to me that he stayed in his marriage given how Jaime treated him. For years, Curt's dedication to caring for Jaime was what kept him going. He maneuvered around his wife's cruel behavior as if it were an inconvenience that did not bother him, but in fact it hurt him deeply. I wondered if Curt had always been this nice or if his perpetual self-doubt, insecurity, and lack of confidence somehow fueled his compassion. The neuroscientific evidence is clear—if you use a brain network often, it grows and fortifies. Few have ever done more for someone than Curt did for Jaime, and as her treatment of him worsened, Curt became kinder and more intensely focused on making Jaime better.

Thoughts about Jaime and Curt raced through my mind as I looked at an MRI of Jaime's brain. The scan suggested that Jaime's symptoms were indeed due to a neurodegenerative disorder and not a stroke, infection, or tumor. In neurodegenerative disorders, atrophy in the brain can be widespread when symptoms are severe, and I had anticipated that there would be significant tissue loss in Jaime's brain given her current state of impairment. My suspicion was correct.

The posterior regions on both sides of Jaime's brain, including the parietal and occipital lobes, were normal in size. This did not surprise me as Jaime did not have major difficulties with navigation or visuospatial processing, symptoms that often arise when these parts of the brain are not functioning well. The anterior regions of the brain, however, showed notable atrophy. In a healthy person, the two hemi-spheres of the brain are usually similar in volume, but in Jaime, there was a noticeable asymmetry between the left and right sides. While the left frontal and anterior temporal lobes were more typical in size, those same structures in the right hemisphere were only slivers of tissue. In fact, it was the most severe and asymmetrical brain atrophy I had ever seen. The parts of the frontal lobes that were the most affected were the right anterior cingulate cortex and the right anterior insula (Figure 2.1). I knew from Dr. Benson that loss of tissue in the frontal and anterior temporal lobes on the right side could have a profound impact upon social behavior, and this seemed to be true for Jaime.

Shifting uncomfortably in his seat, Curt waited patiently for me to speak. I suspected that he knew that I had seen something ominous on the MRI. I was ready to tell Curt Jaime's diagnosis. The story he told, together with my own observations and her MRI, suggested that the behavioral variant of FTD was the neurodegenerative disorder from which she suffered.

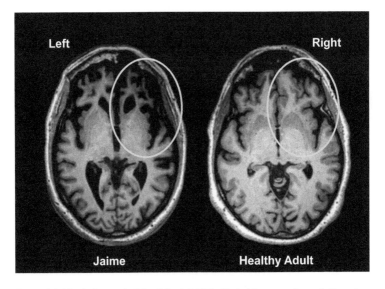

Figure 2.1 The dark areas in Jaime's brain MRI indicated there was dramatic tissue loss in the anterior regions of the right hemisphere. The atrophy in Jaime's brain is notable when her scan is contrasted with that of a healthy adult, which has more gray areas that indicate intact tissue.

FTD is a family of neurodegenerative disorders that affects behavior and language (Figure 2.2). In contrast to individuals with Alzheimer's disease, who often exhibit their first symptoms in their late sixties, seventies, or eighties, people with FTD often develop symptoms before the age of 65. There are three different clinical variants of FTD that reflect the parts of the frontal and temporal lobes that are most affected. People with the behavioral variant of FTD exhibit dramatic shifts in personality, emotions, and social behavior due to pronounced changes in the frontal and anterior temporal lobes. Often, these changes are more pronounced in the right hemisphere than in the left. When FTD targets the left hemisphere, people develop a primary progressive aphasia. Primary progressive aphasias are disorders of language and speech that make it difficult for people to understand or produce speech. FTD can cause two types of primary progressive aphasia. When the disease targets the anterior temporal lobes, people are diagnosed with a semantic variant that is characterized by loss of semantic knowledge. When the disease affects the left frontal lobe, people are diagnosed with a non-fluent variant, which is notable for impairments in speech production and grammar.

In the behavioral variant of FTD, the first areas of dysfunction in the frontal lobes are usually the anterior cingulate cortex and the anterior insula.[41] The anterior cingulate cortex, a region that lies along the midline of the frontal

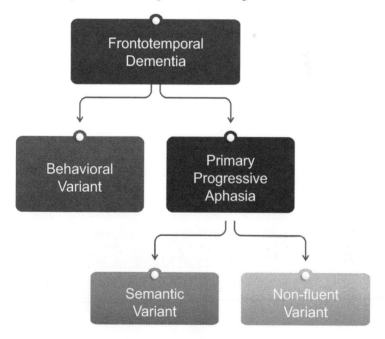

Figure 2.2 FTD refers to a family of syndromes that can affect behavior and language.

lobes, plays a key role in emotion generation and motivation. When we feel slighted, rebuffed, or excluded by others, the anterior cingulate cortex and anterior insula activate.[42] While the anterior cingulate cortex triggers the changes in the body that arise during emotions, the anterior insula (Latin for "island") allows us to become aware of these changes. The anterior insula, an area tucked deep between the frontal and temporal lobes, receives continuous signals from the organs and muscles that influence our experience and behavior. The anterior cingulate cortex and anterior insula not only activate during emotions, but they also respond to other important states such as pain, temperature, hunger, and thirst.[43] By facilitating our ability to produce and sense our own emotions, the anterior cingulate cortex and anterior insula also enable us to feel others' emotions and to have empathy (Figure 2.3).

When FTD targets the anterior cingulate cortex and anterior insula in the right hemisphere, as was the case for Jaime, people no longer generate or experience fear, sadness, disgust, and embarrassment, negative emotions that prompt us to withdraw and avoid. Losing these emotions can be dangerous as people with the behavioral variant of FTD can no longer detect threats to their safety or health. Without fear, they put themselves in harm's way, and without disgust, they eat spoiled food without noticing that may be exposing themselves to harmful contamination. Indeed, it was uncommon for Jaime to display these negative emotions as her illness progressed. As anger relies more on circuits in the left hemisphere, the relative preservation of left frontal and anterior temporal regions in Jamie may have protected, or even heightened, her ability to produce and experience anger as other negative emotions degraded. Jaime also had atrophy in the orbitofrontal cortex, another part of the frontal lobes that helps us to regulate our emotions. Atrophy in this region may have made it difficult for her to hold back her feelings of anger when they arose.

Jaime could still produce and experience anger, but she did not seem to care if her actions angered others. Families of people with the behavioral

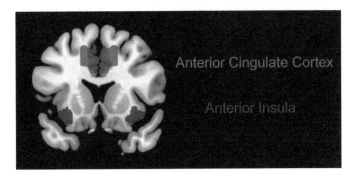

Figure 2.3 The anterior cingulate cortex and anterior insula.

variant of FTD often note that their loved one no longer acts in considerate ways and no longer takes their thoughts and feelings into account. In our research, we have found that they may act in these ways, in part, because they have a diminished appreciation of fairness. In one study, people with the behavioral variant of FTD won a small amount of money as they played a game on a computer.[44] Next, we told them that, if they chose to do so, they could give money to a stranger who was also playing the game. We reassured them that giving to the other person would not impact how much money they would keep. The healthy controls in our study usually offered money to the stranger because, why not? They themselves did not benefit financially from giving money but giving just seemed fair and right. Those with the behavioral variant of FTD did not have this drive, however. They were less inclined to give money to the stranger even though they could have done so without penalty. It did not matter to them if it was fair or not.

To be fair, one must know what is equitable in a situation and care enough to make sure that this standard is upheld. Some people with the behavioral variant of FTD know what is right but still act in ways that defy social expectations. There can be a disconnect between the knowledge that they have about what is right and the extent to which they feel motivated to act accordingly. Fairness also relies on empathy, an ability that allows us to recognize and feel how another person feels when treated unfairly. Part of what motivates us to be fair is that being kind activates reward systems in the brain that produce positive emotions. Doing nice things for others makes them—and us—feel good. Neurologist David Perry has found that people with the behavioral variant of FTD have alterations in the brain's reward systems. In some people, the reward systems overreact to substances such as alcohol and cigarettes, which makes it easier for them to develop addictions.[45] Their reward systems no longer respond to social cues such as the feelings of other people, however. For most of us, social interactions elicit positive emotions such as affection, admiration, and gratitude. For people with the behavioral variant of FTD, interacting with others does not elicit these positive feelings and leaves them unmotivated to please others by being kind.[46] The feelings of mutual joy that typically arise between two people when one experiences a win are nonexistent in the behavioral variant of FTD.

As the anterior cingulate cortex and anterior insula decline in the behavioral variant of FTD, most people become less concerned about other people. In Jaime, it seemed these circuits in her social brain had never functioned optimally, and she had never treated others all that well. It was difficult, therefore, to pinpoint exactly when her disease began. As Jaime's illness progressed, some of her behaviors became more extreme, but not altogether different from her actions in high school and college. The feelings and needs of other people rarely influenced Jaime or her decisions; she prioritized her own desires more than anything else—and always had. Jaime's brain wiring in early life may have made her prone to put herself first, but her insensitivity worsened as she aged. She no longer cared about fairness, and she had no qualms about leaving Curt to clean up her messes. Neurologist Zachary Miller's research suggests that our brain organization in childhood helps to explain how neural networks change in the setting of a neurodegenerative disorder in later life.[47] Our least developed circuits are the most vulnerable to decline when neurodegeneration strikes, and for Jaime, these circuits were in her social brain.

As I sat and listened to Curt tell Jaime's story, one thought kept bothering me. Where did Jaime's personality end and her disease begin? It was hard to separate her early struggles with relationships from her later challenges in this domain. From the time she was in high school, Jaime already lacked social sensitivity. Although Jaime was unusually extraverted, she was also cold. She pursued whatever she wanted and was unbothered by how her actions affected others. These traits did not hinder, and perhaps even helped, Jaime's success in early adulthood as she started and managed her own business. With each passing decade, her behavior became more extreme, making it almost impossible for her to interact with others without Curt's support and, later, supervision.

Like many other caregivers, Curt blamed himself for his loved one's decline, yet nothing was further from the truth. He asked me if the antidepressants or sleeping pills that Jaime took could have caused her behavioral symptoms. He also worried that he could have stopped Jaime's illness if only he had sought medical attention earlier. I tried to reassure Curt that her medicines were not the reason Jaime was changing and that neither he, nor anyone else, could have protected her from the powerful biology of FTD.

Curt asked me whether Martha's emotional distance with Jaime could be to blame. Jaime had trouble forming close connections with others even in childhood, and it is likely that distant family relationships exacerbated the vulnerabilities in her social brain. Martha was not an engaged or emotionally available mother. While I believed Martha's parenting style was important to understanding Jaime's behavior as a youth, I was sure that it did not *cause* her disease.

As I learned from Curt, Martha's life was like Jaime's in many ways. Curt told me that, starting in her forties, Martha suffered a steady decline that included business failures and lawsuits. She spent several years in jail after she was found guilty of burning down her factory for insurance money. Eventually, Martha was diagnosed with Alzheimer's disease and died an early death in a nursing home. I thought her behaviors sounded more characteristic of the behavioral variant of FTD than

Alzheimer's disease, but misdiagnosis was the rule, not the exception, at that time.

It seemed to me that Jaime and Martha had similar weaknesses in youth and adulthood. Behavior is complex and multifaceted, but I wondered whether something about their shared biology could have caused their similar personality traits. Was it possible that both mother and daughter had a genetic mutation that interfered with the development and maintenance of the social brain?

We do not know why most people with the behavioral variant of FTD acquire the illness. Some studies suggest that environmental toxins, autoimmune disorders, head injuries, and prior psychiatric illnesses play a role in determining who develops FTD. These variables, as well as many others, increase the risk for neurodegenerative disorders, but for most individuals the cause (or causes) remain unknown. If life experiences do not explain why many people develop the behavioral variant of FTD, we must look to genetics to help account for their symptoms.

In other neurodegenerative disorders (such as Alzheimer's disease) and psychiatric illnesses (such as schizophrenia and autism spectrum disorders), multiple genes play a role in who develops symptoms. Some neurological conditions are due to a mutation in a single gene that causes an entire suite of behavioral, cognitive, and motor problems. This type of inherited genetic mutation can pass from generation to generation, and multiple people in a family show similar symptoms. When Jaime became ill, there was no known genetic mutation that caused FTD, but researchers had described families where the disease had occurred across multiple generations. From Jaime and Martha's family history, it was clear that many of their relatives had similar plights.

Not surprisingly, Curt was much closer to Jaime's family than she was. Over the past few years, he had diligently worked with them to construct her family tree. Everything that Curt did for Jaime was precise and detailed, and his efforts at genealogy were no different. As Curt relayed the histories of Jaime's family members, I realized that multiple people across the generations of her family struggled with similar symptoms. Various relatives were diagnosed with neurological or psychiatric disorders or passed away in middle age with problems that suggested they may have had a neurodegenerative disorder.

From what Curt gathered, Jaime's life story resembled the experiences of her mother, uncle, aunt, and maternal grandfather. In addition to Martha, who had significant behavioral changes, Martha's brother had been diagnosed with a progressive aphasia, a form of FTD that disrupts speech and language. Martha's sister also died in midlife at a mental institution, and her father died relatively young, in his late fifties. He had been diagnosed with an "organic brain syndrome," a non-specific (and outdated) label given to people with cognitive or behavioral changes due to an unknown brain disease. Given the number of people in Jaime's family with behavioral and cognitive symptoms, I suspected that the disease that ran in her family, FTD, was not only heritable but was likely caused by a mutation in a single gene. I did not know which one, however.

Fifteen years after Jaime developed FTD, scientists discovered the genetic mutation that caused her illness. As suspected, a mutation in a single gene was responsible for the disease that affected Jaime and many of her other family members. The mutation that afflicted Jaime and her family was in the progranulin gene, which is critical for the healthy functioning of the frontal and anterior temporal lobes.[48] Mutations in other genes that also cause FTD have since been discovered. These genetic mutations are the culprit behind numerous stories of families shattered and misunderstood. Many of the genetic mutations that cause FTD not only influence the brain as it ages, but in some instances, they also affect how the brain develops. Jaime's unusual brain organization set her apart and allowed her to see the world in ways that differed from other people. Disinterested in others' opinions and criticisms, Jaime could be calculating in her business deals and decisions, a trait that fueled her professional success. Her lack of fairness and generosity, however, impacted her ability to form close relationships and left her without any loyal friends. Only Curt was there to pick up the pieces of Jaime's life when things went wrong.

It was not only the genetic mutation that shaped Jaime's social brain circuitry, but her life experiences were also crucial. Our genes, though once considered static records of our genetic blueprint, are ever-changing just like our brains. While genes establish the basic organization of the social brain, our experiences continue to shape its functioning over the course of our lives. As we navigate different events, our experiences cause chemical changes that activate or deactivate parts of the genome—turning nurture into nature, and nature into nurture—a link that is impossible to separate. When human children have unmet physical or emotional needs, they may develop persistent cognitive and behavioral challenges and differences in social brain organization.[49] Throughout childhood and adolescence, other chronic stressors such as pollution, economic hardship, and adversity also affect social brain development.[50] Studies of other species have revealed similar results. Neuroscientist Michael Meaney found rat pups who were licked and groomed more frequently were less fearful when separated from their mothers than those who received fewer licks.[51] These behavioral tendencies were enduring, and as adults, the rats who had more nurturing interactions as pups could better tolerate stressful events than those who had experienced less early physical contact. Subsequent studies have found comparable results in a wide range of species—even in bumblebees![52] Taken together, these studies suggest that living in environments that foster physical and mental health is critical for the development of our social brain circuitry.

So, in some ways, Curt was probably right. While Jaime had a genetic mutation that weakened the development of her social brain circuits, Martha's emotional neglect made these systems even more fragile. Curt blamed Martha for Jaime's symptoms and believed that the way Martha treated Jaime was unjust. Although Curt was rarely angry at Jaime, he was certainly angry on her behalf. When we think someone that we care about has been wronged, we can experience strong feelings of moral outrage. This type of anger may have driven Curt to provide Jaime with the love that she had lacked in childhood and to overlook her hurtful behaviors. From Jaime's family tree, it was almost certain that Martha—as well as Martha's father and multiple other relatives—all carried the same genetic mutation as Jaime. Martha, too, was born with a biological makeup that made it difficult for her to form and maintain bonds with others. A poor relationship with her own father, who also struggled in similar ways, may have further weakened the vulnerable social circuits that Martha herself inherited. This cycle, driven by both genes and environment, went on and on across the generations of their family, an ongoing dance between nature and nurture that only made the reasons for their social behavior more complex.

Nurturing experiences at any time in life bolster the circuits in the social brain and make them more robust, and there was no doubt that Curt's devotion benefited Jaime. As Jaime's behavior worsened, Curt maintained a ferocious loyalty to her. He protected and cared for the woman he loved for most of his life without asking for anything in return. There was a biological reason for Jaime's behavior, but Curt was harder to understand. The social circuits in Curt's brain might always have been unusually robust, but his life experiences, such as spending time in the Navy as a loyal service member who looked after his comrades, may have further strengthened his social brain networks. There are rare (and wonderful) people like Curt who experience unfairness but rise above their feelings to protect the weak and vulnerable. Curt's compassion made him an outlier in the best way possible, motivating him to care for Jaime and to preserve her dignity throughout her grueling illness.

While Curt had heroic qualities, Jaime was not a villain. Although FTD left Jaime disconnected from the social world, she, too, was a hero in many ways. Jaime also experienced injustices in her life. It was neither fair that she inherited a genetic mutation that would lead to her gradual demise nor that she grew up in a home without love or affection. Despite the weaknesses in Jaime's social brain, she achieved much and had many successes. We all focus on our needs, but Jaime's brain made her more self-absorbed than other people. This self-centeredness may have persisted because it served her well in some ways such as helping her to cope with unwanted feelings of loneliness in her childhood and to make shrewd business decisions that led to her ultimate success.

Like the heroes and villains in Martha's board game and their endless battles between good and evil, networks in our social brains also compete for attention. We feel a push and pull between our own needs and the needs of others, and we each must find a balance between these forces that seems fair and allows us to thrive. The desire to be fair comes, in part, from empathy, and it was this ability that Jaime and Martha lacked.

3 Empathy

As highly social creatures, humans spend their lives cultivating bonds with others. To build social connections, we must understand how others think and feel and anticipate the actions that they may take. From our most casual social interactions—visiting a restaurant, riding a bus, buying groceries—to our long-lasting relationships, we must comprehend the internal worlds of others. Empathy is the foundation of all relationships.

We cannot directly see into other people's minds, but empathy allows us to discern their perspectives and emotions with a high degree of accuracy. By putting ourselves "in their shoes," we can think like they think, or we can vicariously share their experiences by recreating their inner worlds in our own bodies.[53] Without realizing it, we may mimic their gestures and facial expressions, and our heartbeats may synchronize. The intonation in our voices may align. As we mirror the other person's inner states and copy their movements, we can better understand their experiences. These shared feelings not only promote empathy but also foster psychological closeness. When we understand what makes others tick, we are more motivated to alleviate their suffering in times of need and to share in their joy in moments of success.

Differences in brain wiring make some keenly aware of interpersonal cues, and empathy for these individuals comes without effort. Others are less attuned to the nuances of the social world and must work harder to understand the feelings of those around them. While we may be born with certain genetic predispositions for empathy, our experiences further reduce or amplify these natural empathic tendencies. Families, teachers, coaches, therapists, and religious leaders play critical roles in encouraging empathy in children from an early age. Although we may differ in how easily we can nurture our empathic abilities, we can improve our capacity for empathy throughout our lives with effort and intention.

As we learned from Jaime's story, loss of fairness and empathy are prominent features of the behavioral variant of FTD. Jaime was born with lower empathy than many people because of a genetic mutation, and she lost the remnants of her empathy circuits as her illness progressed. Unlike Jaime, most people with FTD do not have a known genetic cause for their symptoms.

DOI: 10.4324/9781003502357-5

Next, we describe Thomas, a man who developed the behavioral variant of FTD for unknown reasons. Thomas had a form of the FTD that targeted the circuits in the social brain that are critical for empathy. As the story of Thomas and his wife, Susan, reveals, even our closest relationships wither when empathy fades.

Dr. Miller's Clinical Note

I met Thomas and his wife, Susan, when they came to their first appointment at our clinic. After a quick round of introductions, we sat down in one of the small examination rooms that lined our clinic's main hallway. Thomas sat bolt upright and remained still as Susan began to relay their story. He stared at me without blinking, his face unexpressive.

Thomas and Susan first met as teenagers while living in a rural town in Northern California. Both hardworking students, Susan was drawn to Thomas's intellect as well as his gentle demeanor. He showed a maturity unlike most others his age and held himself to high moral standards. Soon after graduating from high school, they married. Gifted in mathematics and engineering, Thomas excelled in the emerging technology field while Susan stayed home and cared for their two young children. Hard work and prayer were constants for this close-knit and thriving family.

Two years before they visited our clinic, Susan noticed that her relationship with Thomas was beginning to crumble. They discussed their struggles in couples therapy but had different perspectives about the reasons for their marital stress. The health professionals sided with Thomas and believed that Susan was unnecessarily critical of her husband. In their opinion, she saw flaws in him that were trivial or even nonexistent. Susan, however, knew that Thomas was no longer the same man she had married.

Turning to Susan, I asked, "Can you give me an example of something Thomas did that made it clear to you that he had changed?"

"Yes, Dr. Miller. There was an incident in the garden that convinced me that something was very wrong with Thomas," Susan replied. She took a deep breath and looked briefly at Thomas. Susan next described an incident that she found so upsetting that it steeled her determination to find a physician who would take her concerns seriously.

It was a sunny afternoon, and Susan was working in her garden. Thomas sat in a lawn chair in a shady part of the yard, quietly watching his wife. As Susan trimmed her rose bushes with her garden shears, she struggled to cut a thicker branch. Suddenly she shrieked, dropped the shears, and gripped her hand. Blood ran down her arm to her elbow, where it seeped into the rolled-up sleeve of her denim shirt. She began to sob. Upon peering at her hand, Susan realized that she had accidentally cut off the tip of her left index finger.

Thomas watched the situation unfold but stayed motionless in his chair. At first, he said nothing, but when Susan's crying became more intense, Thomas yelled at her to stop. His reaction shocked Susan, but through tears she urged him to bring her to the hospital. After a long pause, Thomas reluctantly agreed. Rather than rush to the car, he walked slowly to his bedroom to find his wallet. He later explained that he needed his wallet to ensure that he had proper identification if the police were to stop him on the way to the hospital.

After retrieving his wallet, Thomas returned to the yard and picked up the garden shears. He then walked to his neighbor's house and rang the doorbell. When the door opened, Thomas said flatly, "Here, you can use these while we are away. We are going to the hospital." After returning home, he got in the car with Susan and pulled out of the driveway. Susan cried throughout the 20-minute car ride, as troubled by Thomas's indifference to her suffering as she was by the unrelenting pain in her finger. Thomas remained unmoved by his wife's predicament and repeatedly chastised her for interrupting his quiet Saturday afternoon and disturbing the neighbors.

As Susan finished telling me her story, she looked at Thomas and then at me. I returned her gaze with a heavy heart, feeling a mixture of sadness and horror. Throughout the story, Thomas remained still in his chair, staring ahead. He appeared unaffected by his wife's distress and only commented, "Susan can be sloppy and careless. I have warned her many times of the consequences of her actions."

For Susan, the mishap in her garden was alarming. Despite Susan's distress, Thomas was unbothered by her suffering, even resentful. What could explain Thomas's bizarre reaction? Pain is comprised of physical as well as "psychic" or "emotional" components, and both types of pain serve important functions. By prompting us to seek medical attention or to nurture what ails us, pain fosters healing. Without pain, we would not know when to withdraw from an activity or allow ourselves to rest and recover. The physical pain that Susan experienced when she cut her finger was automatic and powerful, but she also felt psychic pain in response to Thomas's indifference. Responding to another person's pain requires empathy, and when someone we love is injured most of us have a strong emotional reaction and desire to help. Thomas, in contrast, felt neither Susan's physical nor emotional pain. Thomas no longer had empathy.

The physical and psychic elements of pain are closely linked, and both activate the insula.[54] As we saw earlier with Jaime, the anterior insula allows us to be aware of our emotions and pain, but this region is not the first area to respond when pain arises. During a painful experience, such as when we touch an object that is hot or sharp, the brain triggers an automatic response. The pain reflex signals danger and allows us to react quickly—to retract our hand if we touch a sizzling pan or to drop a pair of garden shears if we cut our finger. Pain emanating from internal sources, like our organs or muscles, alerts us to potential threats inside the body. No matter the source, sensory information about the threat travels from the body to the brain where it passes through various regions before it heads to the insula. Within the insula, there are different subregions that serve different functions. Just as a thermometer tells you your body temperature by measuring its heat in degrees, the posterior insula maps objective sensory information about the stimulus itself. This part of the insula sticks to the facts and is agnostic to your opinions. When it comes to temperature, activity in the posterior insula increases as each degree climbs higher. Likewise, a deep cut on your finger by a sharp set of shears activates the posterior insula more than a nick with a dull butterknife.

After activating the posterior insula, pain signals travel onward to the anterior insula. The anterior insula is where objective sensory information comingles with our beliefs, knowledge, personality, goals, and memories to create our lived experiences. Compared to the physical components of pain, which travel from the peripheral injury up to the cortex via specific pathways in the body, the emotional aspects are more enigmatic. Our experiences of temperature, pain, and other sensations are not just objective readouts of the facts, and different people can have varying reactions to an identical stimulus or situation. For some, 85 degrees Fahrenheit is ideal for an afternoon outside, but for others, that temperature is sweltering, and they prefer a crisp 65 degrees. The same is true for our emotional experiences in that the same event might be more intense for some people than others.

The anterior insula not only allows us to feel our own emotions and pain, but it also helps us to empathize with others. Neuroscientist Tania Singer conducted pioneering research on empathy by studying pain in romantic couples. In one study, couples came to the laboratory for a research visit.[55] While one partner sat in a chair, the other laid in a functional MRI scanner and had their brain activity measured. During the task, one person in each couple (the participant in the scanner or their partner in the chair) received a painful stimulus—a mild electric shock—on their hand. The results were astounding. The posterior insula only activated when the person in the scanner received the shock, but the anterior insula activated when either the person *or* their partner was in pain. The anterior insula responded to the emotional and cognitive elements of pain, but not the physical pain itself. These results suggest that the anterior insula helps us to experience others' feelings vicariously and that, without this part of the brain, we cannot share another person's internal states. Could Thomas's declining empathy be due to a problem in the anterior insula? (Figure 3.1)

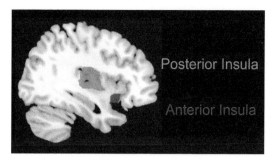

Figure 3.1 The posterior and anterior insula.

From Susan's story, it was clear that Thomas did not empathize with the excruciating pain that she experienced after cutting her finger. His loss of empathy was so dramatic that I was certain there was a massive change in his brain. I started my exam with the traditional tools of neurology and neuropsychology, which allowed me to assess Thomas's physical and cognitive abilities. But I knew these tests would not capture his primary deficits in empathy.

As expected, Thomas's neurological examination confirmed that his motor and sensory functioning were normal. When I pricked him with a pin, he felt discomfort like anyone else would, which confirmed he could still experience physical pain. I prefer to work with others rather than to see patients alone, as each person offers a distinct perspective and can help to generate novel ideas and creative solutions to challenges.

Next, I sent Thomas to see my colleague, Joel Kramer, for cognitive testing to determine whether Thomas had difficulty with specific areas of thinking. Verbal memory, executive functioning, drawing, mathematical calculations, language comprehension, and speech production were all normal. The few areas of cognitive weakness that Thomas displayed were remarkably subtle. He had difficulty naming uncommon objects, such as "lattice," "doorknob," and "octopus," and he struggled to remember the details of a figure that he had copied. But these were minor mistakes in an otherwise robust performance. In fact, Thomas did so well on our tests that some members of our team began to doubt my suspicions that he suffered from a neurodegenerative disorder.

Had his previous health care providers been correct? Were his problems not neurological after all? I had expected Thomas to do well on the standard cognitive tests, but I had not realized just how well he would do. Satisfactory performance on these tests did not rule out an underlying neurodegenerative disorder, however, because they did not evaluate the parts of the brain that I hypothesized were most affected. Although Susan provided numerous examples of clear empathy loss in Thomas, we had few tools that allowed us to quantify his impairments in this area. We needed to assess additional areas of functioning that were more closely associated with empathy, such as his ability to recognize emotions in other people.

To have empathy, we must first recognize that another person is experiencing an emotion. Emotions are accompanied by feelings that others cannot see, but they are not completely impenetrable to others. We send information about our inner states to other people with our face, voice, posture, and actions. These behaviors promote rapid communication and do not rely on language or even close physical proximity. If we see someone across a dark parking lot who looks afraid, we gain important knowledge about a potential threat to them (and to us) even though we have not spoken a word. The face is critical for this type of nonverbal communication. A single raised eyebrow can signal inquisitiveness; a wink, playfulness; and a nose wrinkle, distaste. Other species also use their faces to communicate. Whereas reptiles, birds, and amphibians lack flexibility in how much they can move their faces, mammals have greater facial mobility. Among mammals, humans and other species who live in larger social groups have a broader repertoire of facial movements than species with a more solitary existence.[56] Compared to wolves, domesticated dogs can move their eyebrows in complex ways that signal affiliation.[57] Horses, too, can communicate various feeling states by flickering their eyelashes and flaring their nostrils. For many species, facial expressions are essential for social living.

Although our emotions tend to arise without much warning, we can manage our feelings via numerous strategies. This is called emotion regulation.[58] We often regulate our emotions intentionally—we go for a run, listen to music, or call a friend—because when we feel down these activities can help us to reduce negative feelings and to restore a positive mindset. We also take steps to create our preferred emotional lives without even realizing it. We might avoid situations where we feel uncomfortable and instead surround ourselves with people who bring us peace. When we do find ourselves in an undesirable situation or an unwanted emotion begins to surface, there are other things we can do to make it better. We can alter which details we notice or how we think about the circumstances, which can help us to have a more positive experience.

We also have the power to shape how we communicate our emotions to others. People differ in how forthcoming they are about broadcasting their feelings to strangers and even to people with whom they are close. Some of us lock our feelings away at all costs, while others are comfortable expressing how they really feel. We begin to develop these habits in early childhood. Our families are the first source of information about how to experience and express our emotions, but we continue to learn about how to manage strong feelings from our friends and teachers. People from different backgrounds have varying ideas about emotions and their value in everyday life, and our cultures teach us important lessons about how we should—or should not— reveal our emotions to others. Around the world, social rules about which emotions to display, and when, vary and shape how people manage their feelings during social interactions.[59]

Despite variation in emotional expressivity, humans can recognize feelings in others because emotions have common features across people and cultures. In the 1960s, Paul Ekman, a psychologist at UCSF, began to investigate whether emotions have a biological component that humans around the world share. To explore this question, he traveled to Papua New Guinea and met with people in isolated communities who had little or no contact with other cultures. Using stories about emotions and photographs of faces displaying emotions (some of them his own), Dr. Ekman found happiness, anger, surprise, sadness, disgust, and fear looked similar in Papua New Guinea and the United States.[60] His research suggested that people around the world make similar facial expressions because emotions have a biological basis and are encoded in our DNA. Dr. Ekman also noted, however, that culture, learning, and experience play important roles in shaping our emotions, especially how and when we display our feelings. Building on his groundbreaking studies, psychologists Michelle Shiota, Belinda Campos, Dacher Keltner, and others have since shown that many more emotions (awe, amusement, compassion, and pride, to name a few) also have predictable signals in the face and body that are produced by the brain in a similar way across individuals.[61]

While we can recognize the emotions of people in other cultures because we have similar expressions, there is inherent variability in this ability as well. Some people are better at cognitive empathy, the ability to name the emotions and perspectives of others. Cognitive empathy may not elicit changes in a person's own experience, but they can use observable cues to identify others' emotions. For example, a downturned mouth and knitted eyebrows often signify feelings of sadness, while smiling and laughter usually communicate feelings of amusement. Assessment of cognitive empathy is straightforward and usually involves asking people to label the emotions of others from their face. In some cases, they may be asked to identify other people's feelings from their voice or bodily movement.

To determine whether Thomas could recognize emotions in other people, I asked Katherine Rankin, a neuropsychologist in our clinic, to evaluate his cognitive empathy. She showed Thomas a series of photographs of emotional faces, just like the ones Dr. Ekman used in his early studies. "What emotion is this person feeling?" Dr. Rankin asked Thomas, pointing to the face on the card and gesturing to a list of options that she then read aloud. "Happy, sad, surprised, angry, frightened, disgusted, or neutral?" After Thomas answered, she recorded his response and turned over the next card.

Thomas completed the task with confidence, but his performance was extremely poor. In fact, his score was no better than chance. He had significant trouble recognizing negative emotions, and although he did slightly better at naming happy faces, he still made unexpected mistakes. From this task it was clear that Thomas's cognitive empathy had declined and that he could not recognize emotions in others. I began to wonder, did he still know what emotions look like at all, even in himself?

"Thomas, show me what you look like when you feel sad," I said. He looked at me blankly with no movement in any of his facial muscles. "Is that a sad face?" I asked.

"That is sad," he confirmed.

"What do you look like when you feel angry?" I continued.

"I do not get angry. I never feel angry. Being angry is wrong," Thomas replied in a monotone voice.

"Just try your best to show me what anger looks like," I encouraged. He looked at me, his expression neutral but with his lips now slightly parted. He did not look angry.

I tried another tack. "When Susan was discussing the recent conflicts in your marriage, she was sad. Did you also feel sad while listening to her story?"

Thomas appeared quizzical. "I don't think she was sad. I was not sad," he responded.

From this impromptu exercise, I realized that Thomas had also lost his knowledge of emotions. If he did not know what emotions looked like in others—or in himself—how could he understand what people were feeling? Whether Thomas could still generate emotions in his body or feel emotions of any kind were questions that we could not answer because our tools were insufficient. We needed to develop a new approach. Assessing these domains was critical for understanding Thomas's illness.

To understand whether Thomas could produce emotions required tools that were not a part of routine clinical assessments. One area that we wanted to evaluate in Thomas was the autonomic nervous system. The autonomic nervous system is a set of highly organized pathways that connect the brain and body. During emotions, the autonomic nervous system triggers rapid changes in the organs and muscles. Although difficult to measure without special equipment, the autonomic nervous system could provide important clues about the nature of Thomas's emotional deficits. If his autonomic nervous system were unresponsive to others' emotions, it would help to explain his lack of empathy.

Although it has long been appreciated that the autonomic nervous system plays a central role in in emotions, much about how this works remains a mystery to this day. Dr. Ekman and his colleague, psychologist Robert Levenson, began to conduct the first research in this area in the 1980s. In some of their early studies, they investigated how movement in the facial muscles related to activity in the autonomic nervous system. They first asked whether simply moving one's face into an expression that arises during emotions, such as a smile, could trigger changes in autonomic nervous system activity and alter the way people feel. To answer this question, they attached sensors to the bodies of healthy adults and asked them to move their facial muscles into specific configurations.[62] The participant moved their face into the precise expression that the researchers had instructed ("Wrinkle your nose, lower your brows, and squint your eyes. Good—now hold it there!") and then held that expression for ten seconds. The participants were never told which emotion they were posing, but after holding a specific expression on their face, they reported experiencing the emotion that they displayed. Drs. Ekman and Levenson reasoned that each facial expression elicits a unique feeling because it triggers a distinct set of physiological and motor changes in the body. They next compared the autonomic nervous system activity— heart rate, breathing, temperature, and sweating—of the participants as they posed the expressions and found each expression triggered a different physiological pattern. These findings challenged longstanding views that the autonomic nervous system responds in similar ways during all emotions and instead suggested that the brain generates different bodily changes during each emotion.

At the time of Thomas's visit, we had begun to investigate emotions in people with neurodegenerative disorders. With neurologists Howard Rosen and Richard Perry, Dr. Levenson created novel ways to evaluate whether Thomas and other people with dementia could still produce and feel emotions. Participants in these studies visited Dr. Levenson's laboratory where they completed a variety of activities. In one task, they watched short film clips that typically elicit amusement, sadness, disgust, and fear while their autonomic nervous system activity, facial behavior, and experience were measured.[63] Although people usually exhibit changes in the body and face while watching the film clips, Thomas was unreactive. In the realm of emotions, he was flat as a pancake.

There are different types of empathy that allow us to soothe and support other people. Emotional empathy is a form of empathy that allows us to share others' feelings without engaging in a complex analysis of what we are thinking. As Dr. Singer's studies of empathy illustrated, emotions and pain travel across people automatically. Without any awareness that we are doing so, our heart may beat in synchrony with their heart, and our facial muscle movements may mimic theirs. If they smile, we smile. If they furrow their brow, we furrow ours. Our brains simulate their internal states and allow us to feel what they feel in our own bodies. These mirroring systems are central to empathy because they enable us to form connections both with people we know well and with strangers we have just met.

With ancient roots, emotional empathy was not only evident in early humans but is also present in other species. Birds in a flock fly away if one startles and takes flight, and chimpanzees copy the play face of other chimpanzees. In humans and other highly social species, these shared experiences also foster prosocial behaviors—actions that prioritize the needs of others over one's own. After an aggressive interaction between two chimpanzees, for example, the combatants touch each other in specific and predictable ways. These consolation behaviors reduce distress, promote reconciliation between the aggressors, and restore a calm milieu within the community.[64] Other species demonstrate prosocial helping behaviors in which individuals aid a comrade when they themselves receive no benefit for doing so. In humans, too, shared feelings motivate prosocial behaviors starting early in childhood.[65]

Emotional empathy can promote cognitive empathy by fostering similar experiences across individuals. When our internal states align with those of others, we can more easily figure out how they are feeling. The opposite is also true, and if we can name how someone is feeling using cognitive empathy, we may find that we also begin to experience their emotion. While cognitive and emotional empathy usually work together in a synergistic fashion, in some people these systems become disconnected. Psychopathy is a good example that illustrates how people can have selective impairment in one form of empathy. While psychopaths are often good at cognitive empathy, their emotional empathy is deficient. They can recognize distress in other people, but it does not produce shared feelings of unease.[66] In fact, they may even take joy in other people's pain, sometimes plotting how to make them suffer more. This combination of traits can be deadly, as psychopaths can detect emotions in others and use this information to their advantage without concern for the other person.

Unlike a psychopath, Thomas had deficits in both types of empathy. His lack of cognitive and emotional empathy made it impossible for him to understand and share Susan's physical and emotional pain when she cut her finger or her sadness when she described the current state of their marriage. Susan knew that Thomas's waning empathy was a departure from the person he once was. If his empathy had indeed declined dramatically, it was unlikely that this change was due to alterations in mood or changes in cognition that are common in aging. Instead, it suggested that Thomas had a neurodegenerative disorder that affected the neural circuits in the social brain that support empathy and emotions, just as Susan suspected.

The assessment in Dr. Levenson's laboratory confirmed that Thomas was no longer able to recognize, produce, or feel emotions, but we still needed to find the underlying cause of his deficits. If a neurodegenerative disorder were the cause of Thomas's problems, his symptoms would have appeared slowly and gradually worsened over time. Many aspects of Thomas's life were the same now as they always had been. He continued to work, drive without difficulty, remember recent events, and fix appliances in the house. Yes, the event in the garden was shocking. And Susan was certain that Thomas had grown distant and was now a different person. To assuage my remaining doubts and to confirm that the changes had worsened over time, I needed to obtain more information about his history.

"Susan, was the incident in the garden the first time you noticed that Thomas had lost empathy?" I inquired.

She shook her head and confirmed that the incident in the garden was merely one in a long series of events in which Thomas displayed waning empathy. Susan noted that over the past few years, he had alienated not only her but also their two daughters, their friends, the pastor at their church, and even their beloved dogs who began to avoid him due to frequent yelling and punishment.

Susan then described another significant event that occurred several years prior, the first time that she began to wonder if there was something wrong with her husband. This incident centered on Margaret, their eldest daughter, who was being bullied at school. After weeks of insults, Margaret yelled at one of her assailants and was sent to the principal's office. The principal disregarded her story about being bullied and put her on one month of probation.

When they went to the school to meet with the principal, Thomas was quick to reprimand, rather than console, his daughter. As she tried to tell her side of the story, he interrupted her and said without feeling, "We follow laws and rules. You can never shout in class or contradict a teacher." Although Susan understood the distress that Margaret experienced at the hands of the bullies, Thomas did not. For him, rules took precedent, and he could not see the situation from her perspective. The parts of his brain that remembered rules, which depend largely on the left hemisphere, were intact, but the brain areas that made emotional sense of those rules no longer worked the way they once did. Thomas's lack of empathy shocked Margaret and created a permanent rift between her and her father.

This story, and others, convinced me that Thomas's empathy had been steadily declining for several years. This slow change was consistent with the gradual progression that we see in neurodegenerative disorders. The final piece of information that I needed to make a diagnosis was an MRI of Thomas's brain. If his symptoms were due to a neurodegenerative disorder, there should be evidence of tissue loss in his brain. Based on his symptoms, I expected that the right anterior areas of the brain would be most affected. I needed to review a brain scan to confirm that this was the case. Luckily, Susan had brought a copy of his recent MRI.

The pattern I saw in the images was distinctive. There was profound but highly focal atrophy in the right hemisphere, especially in the anterior portions. The regions most affected were the right anterior insula and the right anterior temporal lobe, with milder atrophy in these same structures on the left side. The amygdala was also nearly absent on the right and notably small on the left. The areas at the back of the brain were intact.

The atrophy pattern in Thomas's MRI confirmed my suspicions and solidified his diagnosis. A neurodegenerative disorder was the cause of Thomas's loss of empathy, and he had a type of the behavioral variant of FTD that attacks the right anterior temporal lobe. I was shocked that this relatively focal damage to the right anterior temporal lobe could lead to such devastating changes in behavior. Susan had been right all along.

In Thomas, there was notable atrophy in areas of the social brain that are critical for empathy (Figure 3.2). He lived in a cocoon devoid of emotions, and tissue loss in the anterior insula made it difficult for Thomas to feel his own emotions let alone anyone else's. Atrophy in the right, more than the left, anterior temporal lobe and amygdala also disrupted his ability to recognize and produce emotions. We now know that the right anterior temporal lobe and amygdala are critical for empathy.[67] The right anterior temporal lobe also stores information, or semantic knowledge, about people and feelings. When the right anterior temporal lobe no longer functions well, as was the case for

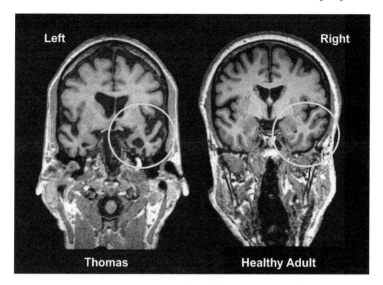

Figure 3.2 The dark spaces in Thomas's brain MRI show right anterior temporal lobe atrophy.

Thomas, people have trouble understanding emotions because they no longer know what emotions look or feel like. Degeneration in these regions interfered with Thomas's ability to share the feelings of his wife and daughters when they were in distress. Without his feelings to guide his thinking and actions, Thomas increasingly relied on old rules that he had learned rather than adapting to each situation as needed.

At the time that Thomas and Susan first visited our clinic, the word "empathy" was rarely used in medicine. In neurology and psychiatry, empathy was discussed occasionally as a psychological phenomenon, but few considered its biological basis. Even today, evaluations of empathy are not a routine part of clinical assessments. None of the medical professionals Thomas saw prior to his UCSF visit believed his empathy decline could be due to a neurological condition, and it was only because of Susan's persistence that they reluctantly referred him to our clinic. Before meeting Thomas, we had never seriously considered how the brain supported empathy, or whether loss of empathy could be the manifestation of a neurodegenerative disorder. We soon discovered that if we did not investigate the biology of empathy, we would never understand the behavioral variant of FTD.

Thomas and Susan became a frequent topic of discussion at our center, and they took part in numerous research projects without hesitation. But how much could we learn from one couple? As Dr. Benson had believed, the simple answer is that we learned an extraordinary amount! Studies of Thomas and others like him brought new insights into the circuitry of empathy. Importantly, loss of empathy even became part of our new diagnostic criteria for the behavioral variant of FTD. Susan and Thomas believed that participating in research is what people should do for society. They did not expect that any of the knowledge we gained from Thomas would benefit him, but they wanted to help others in the future. Their long-held religious beliefs brought out a generosity and selflessness in both Thomas and Susan that was extraordinary. Thomas had lost the systems in the social brain that allowed him to know what others are feeling, and he reacted to them with coldness, even cruelty. Nevertheless, he maintained his longstanding belief that he should help others and tried to embody a value system that, in many ways, made him exemplary.

There are still many unanswered questions about empathy. Who can change and who cannot? And what can we learn from the outliers in empathy like Thomas? If some people have super-empathy and improve many lives, why do others lack empathy and focus their energy on hate, disparaging people with different skin colors, religions, and politics? And what about societies that abandon empathy, at least temporarily, during campaigns of aggression? While these questions were once the purview of the social sciences and philosophy, these issues now fall in the domain of neuroscience.

4 Respect

A society tends to prosper when its citizens respect common codes of conduct. People do not have carte blanche to act however they wish, and laws and social rules encourage them to avoid actions that are unfair or harmful to others. Laws exist for a reason, and legal expectations are often very clear. We follow the rules of the road while driving, we tell the truth in a court of law, and we pay for items at a store. Individuals obey these laws for one of two reasons: they hold themselves to a high moral standard, or they want to avoid punishment. Sometimes, a bit of both keeps us on the straight and narrow.

Social rules can be more ambiguous. We respect others' property and do not use their belongings without permission. We appreciate their personal space and are mindful of how we make eye contact. But there are no exact specifications for where to draw these lines, and we learn as we go. In everyday life, we navigate numerous environments, and as such, we must incorporate many sets of expectations. For our interactions to be successful, we must follow the social rules that apply to that setting. We ensure that our behavior is appropriate by monitoring the social context and tracking our actions to minimize missteps.

The social rules that guide us are especially complex. Social rules are context-dependent and can vary across people, contexts, and cultures. Some cultures have complex rituals to demonstrate respect to others, particularly to elders and figures of authority. In Korean culture, for example, the social hierarchy is a key element of drinking rituals. When people are with their colleagues or bosses, they must pour and receive drinks with both hands whenever possible, and the people with higher status drink first. When a person with higher status wants to toast others in the group, those of lower status must ensure their glasses remain below the more senior person's glass when their glasses clink. The toasting rules immediately change if the higher status person leaves. After the senior person's departure, each person in the group updates their perceived status and adjusts the position they assume when clinking glasses in subsequent toasts. Not making this rapid adjustment is a sign of disrespect to the others. Many other cultures do not have these types of drinking rituals, and a person unfamiliar with these rules would need to learn them to avoid making a social faux pas.

DOI: 10.4324/9781003502357-6

Figure 4.1 Tablets outlining the Code of Hammurabi.

Human societies have long grappled with how to communicate social rules and to maintain social order. Nearly 2,000 years ago, humans began to codify their society's rules and laws in writing. Some of the earliest known legal texts were created by Hammurabi, the king of Babylon, who ordered the laws of his ancient society to be carved into a huge stone slab, visible for all to see. The Code of Hammurabi provided detailed guidelines about how citizens should manage issues pertaining to family, property, commerce, and crime. These rules encouraged a just and orderly society (Figure 4.1).

To respect the social rules, there must be a balance between the brain circuits that tell us to go and the brain circuits that tell us to stop. Rewards and punishments compete for our attention and influence our behavior. While ancient systems deep in the brain encourage us to act on our desires and reach our goals, other circuits hold us back and prevent us from making mistakes. The frontal lobes are the calculator that performs the cost-benefit analysis for each of our actions. When the areas of the frontal lobes that restrain people from acting do not function well, they may no longer behave in ways that respect society's rules and laws.

Clark is an example of such a case. For most of his life, he followed legal and social expectations. In midlife, changes in his frontal lobes left him unable to control his impulses. As is often true in people with these types of neurological changes, trouble soon followed.

Dr. Miller's Clinical Note

It was early in the morning when my office phone rang. When I picked up the receiver, a woman with a delicate Southern drawl greeted me. She spoke rapidly and in a hushed voice.

"Dr. Miller, my name is Ellen Marion. My lawyer suggested that I call you because I am desperate, and I don't know what to do." Before I could respond, she pressed on.

"My husband, Clark, is in serious trouble. Three months ago, he was arrested for driving under the influence, speeding, and fleeing from an officer. He was driving 90 miles per hour in a 25-mile-per-hour zone. When the police signaled to him to pull over, he fled. Eventually, he stopped and surrendered. Clark failed the field sobriety test, and when checked, his blood alcohol level was twice the legal limit. At the police station, Clark took a swing at the police officer, which added assault to his list of charges. This is just totally unlike him. This is not the man I married, Dr. Miller. Clark was born a Yankee, but he has always been a perfect gentleman!"

My eyes widened as I appreciated her unexpected joke. She added, "You know I am just kidding about the Yankee part. He was always a gentleman, even when he lived up north." Ellen is funny, I thought to myself. She had admirable grace in the setting of this unfortunate situation.

"Sorry, I know I am being rude. I haven't given you a chance to talk," she said and then suddenly burst into tears. I sat quietly on the line as she gathered herself. She recovered quickly. "Sorry, I'm just desperate for help."

"Oh no—I am the one who is sorry. This is a terrible situation. Tell me more—I will do anything I can to help," I assured her.

At the time of his arrest, everyone, including Ellen, assumed that drinking was the source of Clark's problems. Alcohol seemed to turn him into a different person. Prior to his arrest, Clark had been a highly respected leader in his community. He was born on the East Coast into a family that was both distinguished and wealthy. While completing his Master's in business administration at an Ivy League school, he met Ellen, who came from a prominent southern family. They soon married and moved near Ellen's family. It was there that Clark established his career and that he and Ellen raised their three children. When he was 50, Clark became president of a local philanthropic organization with a huge budget. He was a charismatic leader who prioritized the needs of his employees and staff. The foundation's board members admired him for his selflessness and interpersonal skills.

When he was 56 years old, three years before his arrest, things began to change for Clark. He started drinking heavily. He began to carry a flask filled with scotch to work, and some days, he had three or four drinks before heading home. Although Clark had always been fastidious, his desk became cluttered, and he required more help from his staff to finish tasks and paperwork.

He came to work with stains on his clothing and his shirttails hanging sloppily outside of his pants, which was very unlike him. In addition, his interactions with people started to change. Clark flirted with his female staff members, and one filed a sexual harassment complaint with the organization. In the months prior to his arrest, Clark was under scrutiny due to his lack of productivity on the job. He had failed to complete his foundation's annual report, which was an unprecedented professional mistake for him. Six months after the report was due, the board members asked Clark when he would have it completed. His response was to offer a middle finger. The press coverage of his arrest was the last straw, and Clark was fired from his job.

By temporarily decreasing the functioning of the frontal lobes, alcohol loosens people and reduces their inhibitions. When consumed in excess over many years, alcohol can have longstanding effects and even cause dementia. Dr. Benson taught me that, contrary to conventional wisdom, alcohol-induced dementia was rare. He also said once people stop drinking, they usually recover unless something else is going on in their brain. Dr. Benson's sayings were almost always right.

After Clark's arrest, he was moved from jail to an alcohol rehabilitation unit. Ellen told me that he quit drinking while he was there, but he started to smoke and chew tobacco. He also gained 60 pounds. He swore profusely and yelled at the staff and other clients whenever he felt like it.

"Could this all be due to alcohol?" Ellen asked. "Did alcohol destroy his mind? He did drink heavily for two years."

My response was noncommittal. "Well, he didn't drink for that long. Maybe it is not the alcohol. Have you seen any improvements in Clark now that he is sober?"

"No, no, he is worse," she said. "I hate those rehab units. They just replace one bad habit with another. He came in abusing alcohol, and the drinking stopped. But now he is smoking, chewing tobacco, and overeating. He yells all the time. I'm scared to have him back home."

It was clear from Ellen's story that Clark had lost his self-control. His desires drove his actions, and he seemed unable to rein them in. Ellen, coworkers, and the police had all been subjected to his wrath, and no one was immune from his insults and disrespect. If Clark's behavior did not improve after he stopped drinking, I thought to myself, then it was unlikely that alcohol was to blame for his current state. There must be another reason. Neurodegenerative disorders, such as FTD, can make people less inhibited, even "disinhibited," by weakening impulse control. I worried that FTD might be the cause of Clark's excessive drinking and misbehavior. As it turned out, Ellen had the same concern.

"He definitely needs a thorough neurological evaluation," I told her. "His legal case may come down to whether Clark knew that he was breaking the law."

We agreed that I would review Clark's medical records, including an MRI of his brain. We also set a date for them to come to my office in California so that the three of us could meet in person. I was confident that I could help with a diagnosis, but I was not sure I could help Clark stay out of jail. I wondered how the laws would be used to determine his culpability.

In the 21st century, the legal guideline that dictates whether someone is accountable for their actions still hinges upon a case from the 1840s. In 1843, Daniel M'Naghten shot and killed the secretary of the British Prime Minister, Edward Drummond, whom he believed was conspiring against him and trying to murder him. During the trial, the jury acquitted Mr. M'Naghten "by reason of insanity," and he spent the rest of his life in a mental institution instead of prison. In the present day, defendants are presumed sane until their lawyers prove that "a disease of the mind" rendered them unable to appreciate the significance of their actions. To invoke the M'Naghten rule, a jury must use the expert medical testimony and the arguments from both sides of the case to decipher a defendant's mental state at the time of the offense.[68] The jury must evaluate whether the defendant knew what they were doing at the time of the crime and whether they knew their actions were wrong. Making this decision about culpability is always difficult. Although written more than a century before the emergence of modern neuroscience, the M'Naghten rule is still the bellwether of legal liability.

Clark's lawyers did not think that they could successfully argue that he was legally insane at the time of his crimes. The extent to which he understood right from wrong, however, was still a key question. If his lawyers could show that Clark did not understand the difference, the judge might reduce his charges.

I met Clark and Ellen in my office one week after our phone call. Ellen was an impeccably dressed, petite woman. For the appointment, she had dressed Clark in a blue blazer, light blue shirt, striped tie, and khaki pants. His shirt, tucked into his pants, was tight and revealed a rounded belly. They were the best dressed people I had ever seen in my clinic.

We sat down to begin the interview. Ellen's eyes glistened with tears as she told Clark's story and described the crimes he had committed. She was bewildered by his behavior and could not understand why he had broken the law. She seemed tense and was careful with her words so as not to upset him. While we talked, he silently played with the pens on my desk. I wondered what he was thinking about.

Once learned, society's rules are hard to erase from the brain as they are encoded by many regions in the left hemisphere. People rarely commit crimes because they do not know the difference between right and wrong. Was it possible that Clark did not know that he had broken the law? I needed to determine if he understood that what he did was wrong. My suspicion was that Clark knew the laws and would not meet M'Naghten criteria for legal insanity.

"Clark, is it legal to drive over the speed limit?" I asked.

"It is illegal to drive over the speed limit," he said.

"And what about drinking and driving... should one do that?" I continued.

"You should not drink and drive," he stated without hesitation. "It is against the law." Ellen and I both nodded. From the corner of my eye, I saw her sink in the chair. She knew the legal implications of what Clark had just said.

As we were nearing the end of the interview, Clark asked if he could eat lunch. I wanted to show them some California hospitality, so we walked over to the crowded medical center cafeteria. As I showed them around, we picked up our trays and went in different directions to find our lunches. Ellen chose tea and a small salad. Clark filled his tray with a large soda, three bacon cheeseburgers, French fries, and four different desserts.

At the cashier, Clark stopped, blocking the path for all the customers. He refused to move. Spotting the barricade that he was creating, Ellen approached Clark and touched his arm, trying to steer him out of the way.

"Don't touch me!" Clark yelled and flung his tray to the ground. A silence filled the cafeteria, and all eyes turned toward Clark, Ellen, and the huge mess on the floor. I immediately understood Ellen's caution around Clark and her fear of upsetting him.

As we walked back to my office, Clark was unapologetic. When I asked him whether it was right to throw food in the cafeteria, he shrugged his shoulders and said, "I shouldn't lose my temper." Ellen looked at him and patted his arm. She and I both knew that Clark's problems were not because he did not know the rules.

Following social rules, though often automatic, is more complicated than it appears. At an early age, we learn the difference between right and wrong. We also learn the consequences for failing to meet social expectations. Children learn how to behave in different settings and how to treat their parents, siblings, friends, and teachers. Some social rules are taught explicitly ("Do not pull your brother's hair!"), but others we discern through trial and error.

A child's understanding of the rules becomes more refined as they get older and gain life experiences. We store social rules and scripts across many regions in our brains and later reference this information when making decisions about how to behave in different contexts.

Some social rules are always true, but sometimes an action can be desirable in one situation but awkward, or even inappropriate, in another. Societies around the world differ in the degree to which they emphasize the needs of the individuals or the society, and these priorities influence their social rules. Individualistic cultures, like the United States, focus on the needs (and the rights) of each person. Collectivist cultures, like many in Asia, value the necessities of the larger group. Even within one country, some social rules vary across regions. They may even differ across towns and cities. In some towns, for instance, residents may bring their dogs into the neighborhood café, but in other towns, that behavior may be frowned upon. Even schools, religious organizations, friend groups, and families create their own unique cultural norms. As we navigate these different environments, we must learn how to behave in each of these contexts by following the relevant social rules. People with FTD break rules in all types of cultures because they lose the capacity to follow the legal and social expectations.

For most of his life, Clark had respected the social rules of his community, which emphasized tact and etiquette. Clark had learned to value all people but particularly elders, women, and authority figures. Ellen also reinforced these principles. Throughout his life, Clark had met, and exceeded, all expectations, and his refined manners were key to his professional success. Clark knew that it was wrong to speed, drive under the influence, hit a police officer, and throw a tray in a cafeteria. So then why would he do these things?

When we returned from the cafeteria, we continued Clark's evaluation. During his time with me, he spoke little and denied any concern about his job loss or pending litigation. Clark expressed love for Ellen but complained that she tried to micro-manage his activities. Over the course of several hours, he ate four packets of sunflower seeds, a new habit that had replaced his tobacco chewing.

Clark cooperated with me as I completed my neurological examination, which did not reveal any areas of impairment. His motor and sensory functions were intact, and his recent blood work was normal. Next, we needed to test Clark's cognitive abilities and to observe his behavior in a structured setting. A meeting with the neuropsychologist, Kyle Boone, would allow us to do both.

During the neuropsychological assessment, Clark was upbeat and did surprisingly well. He had no trouble on tests of language, visuospatial processing, or episodic memory. His performance on tests of executive functioning, however, was a different story. Most notably,

Clark had difficulty on a task that required him to draw as many unique designs as he could in a short amount of time. He had to follow two simple rules. Each design needed to be different and could only use five lines. He made multiple mistakes and repeated many of his designs two, three, and even four times. He broke the rules but did not seem to notice.

After Clark completed this test, Dr. Boone checked to confirm that he had indeed understood and remembered the instructions. "Clark, do you recall how many lines you were supposed to use in each of your designs?"

"Five lines. And each should be different," Clark answered before adding with a grin, "You look young. How about we get dinner sometime? I bet your boyfriend won't mind." He kept smiling as Dr. Boone turned away without responding.

I did not think Clark's past alcohol use explained his executive functioning deficits and inappropriate social behavior. Instead, his slowly progressing symptoms suggested that he suffered from a neurodegenerative disorder. The changes in Clark were consistent with those that we see in the behavioral variant of FTD. I expected that he would have prominent atrophy in the frontal lobes. As I reviewed a copy of his recent brain MRI, suspicions were confirmed. Clark had severe atrophy in the anterior areas of the brain. Within the frontal lobes, the most prominent tissue loss was in the medial and lateral orbitofrontal cortex, extending back into the anterior cingulate cortex. The back of the brain was normal.

Interestingly, M'Naghten was not the only famous case from the 1840s that was relevant to Clark's story. In 1848, physician John Harlow described the tragic story of a railroad worker, Phineas Gage, who suffered a terrible brain injury.[69] One day at work, Mr. Gage was preparing explosives to blast rock in an area where they were building a railroad. As he tamped the blasting powder with a large iron rod, a spark triggered an explosion. The iron rod shot upward and into his head where it destroyed his orbitofrontal cortex, the lower part of the frontal lobes that lies right behind the eyes.[70] Mr. Gage somehow survived this catastrophic incident. In the years that followed, his memory and day-to-day functioning remained intact, but his social behavior was never the same. Once polite and demure, he became irreverent, profane, and obstinate. Dr. Harlow noted that after his injury, Mr. Gage had the "animal passions of a strong man" and was "impatient of restraint or advice when it conflicts with his desires." Like Clark, Mr. Gage's respect for social rules disappeared, and he now acted on his impulses and showed "but little deference for his fellows."

The orbitofrontal cortex functions like a set of traffic lights that guides behavior. By integrating various streams of information, the brain evaluates the pros and cons of acting in each situation. The orbitofrontal cortex is essential for this calculation. The medial orbitofrontal cortex, a subregion that surrounds the brain's midline between the eyes, is like a green light that tells us to put our foot on the gas—to go, to act. This region activates when we determine that a stimulus is rewarding to us in that moment.[71] There are many things that people find rewarding in life—food, alcohol, money, etcetera. Positive social exchanges such as a smiling face, warm hug, or kind words from a friend are also rewarding and activate the medial orbitofrontal cortex.

While rewards may be alluring, humans can resist temptation because of these complex networks in the frontal lobes. In many animals, rewarding stimuli elicit specific innate behaviors that are difficult to inhibit. Ethologist Nikolaas Tinbergen noted that when chicks see seeds on the ground, they peck; when bees detect certain flowers, they land; and when dogs smell food, they eat.[72] Try to convince your dog to ignore the food in their bowl if they are hungry. It is possible for them to control the impulse to eat, but only after significant training. Without sophisticated frontal lobes, animals have a limited ability to override their impulses.

In humans, the lateral orbitofrontal cortex, which is in the lower part of the frontal lobes at the sides of the brain, is like the yellow and red lights in the traffic signal. This area tells us to proceed with caution or to put on the brakes.[73] By tracking the potential negative consequences of our behavior, this region helps us to adjust our actions in response to feedback from the environment. The lateral orbitofrontal cortex and the anterior insula are in close communication with the dorsolateral prefrontal cortex, the area of the frontal lobes near the top of the head at the brain's surface. The dorsolateral prefrontal cortex allows us to consider our actions in a broader context and to reflect on the long-term consequences of our choices (Figure 4.2).

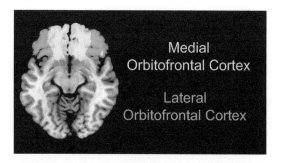

Figure 4.2 Medial and lateral orbitofrontal cortex.

The orbitofrontal cortex has a complicated job because rewards, just like beauty, are in the eye of the beholder. Even what we consider to be rewarding is not fixed and can change in an instant. Our food preferences are a good example of how this works. Neuroscientist Dana Small found that when we are hungry, eating chocolate is gratifying and activates the medial orbitofrontal cortex and connected reward systems.[74] When we are full, however, chocolate loses its appeal. We want to stop eating chocolate when the lateral orbitofrontal cortex and anterior insula begin to trigger feelings of distaste. Studies of non-human primates have found comparable results. Neuroscientists Hugo Critchley and Edmund Rolls discovered the medial orbitofrontal cortex activated when hungry monkeys saw or smelled bananas. After the monkeys had eaten their fill and were offered more bananas, the medial orbitofrontal cortex stopped responding and the lateral orbitofrontal cortex took over.[75] The researchers observed that these regions were not involved in evaluating the physical characteristics of the chocolate and bananas because these properties did not change. The orbitofrontal cortex was only critical for gauging the relative value of these foods as the humans and monkeys transitioned from hungry to full. As the traffic lights in the orbitofrontal cortex shift from green to yellow to red, stimuli turn from desirable to aversive.

Any dysfunction in the orbitofrontal cortex creates havoc in the brain's traffic light system. The orbitofrontal cortex not only uses internal cues from the body, but it also incorporates social information. People's reactions to our behavior provide us with important feedback about whether we have made a social miscalculation. By tracking this social information, the orbitofrontal cortex alerts us to adjust our behavior. In Mr. Gage, a terrible accident with an iron rod injured his orbitofrontal cortex and caused him to disregard social rules for the rest of his life. After his brain injury, Mr. Gage no longer knew when he had committed a social transgression.

Damage to the orbitofrontal cortex can arise for other reasons. In the behavioral variant of FTD, the orbitofrontal cortex is often an early site of atrophy, as was the case for Clark. After his disease began, he did not notice others' displeased reactions to his misbehavior. Ellen's stories and Clark's performance on cognitive testing made it clear that he was no longer tracking his actions. On the task where Clark was asked to draw as many unique designs as he could, he drew without concern for the rules, and as a result, he made many mistakes. In her research, neuropsychologist Katherine Possin has since found the people who make errors on this test tend to have atrophy in the lateral frontal lobes, including the lateral orbitofrontal cortex.[76] On this test, just like in everyday life, it is more effortful to monitor one's actions and to make sure one is following the rules. Clark no longer noticed if he was staying in line with expectations.

Despite the ease with which the orbitofrontal cortex usually conducts its computations, sometimes we still unintentionally break social rules. Luckily, the brain has a back-up plan. Self-conscious emotions—that is, embarrassment, shame, and guilt—arise when we have made a mistake and feel that we have failed to live up to the expectations of others.[77] Embarrassment typically arises after we realize we have committed a faux pas. When we are embarrassed, our heart rate speeds up, our hands sweat, and our cheeks blush. We display predictable behaviors including averting our eyes and looking down, trying to control our smile, and touching our face or neck (Figure 4.3).[78] Although unpleasant to experience, embarrassment serves important social functions. Embarrassment signals to others that we value their opinions and our relationships with them and prompts us to apologize for our mistakes.

If Clark were aware of his mistakes, he was not embarrassed and did not seem to care. Not surprisingly, he was unapologetic for his actions. In our studies, we have found embarrassment is an emotion that is particularly vulnerable in the behavioral variant of FTD. Because embarrassment is hard to measure in the real world, we studied a group of people with the behavioral variant FTD and a comparison group of healthy older adults in Dr. Levenson's emotions laboratory.[79] They completed a karaoke task and sang along to the song, "My Girl," while we videotaped them. Without warning, we showed them the video that we had just recorded of them singing the song. To make

Figure 4.3 Example of a person displaying embarrassment. Photograph used with permission by Sarah Holley.

it more embarrassing, there was no background music in the video, just their own voice. As they watched, we measured their heart rate, sweating, and breathing. We later coded their facial behavior. For many in the healthy group, watching themselves sing elicited intense embarrassment. They laughed, looked away, blushed, and groaned as they observed their performance. Their heart rate increased and so did the sweatiness of their hands. The people with the behavioral variant of FTD, however, showed none of these responses. Instead, they simply watched the video, unaffected by how they came across in this unexpected and ridiculous situation.

To identify the parts of the brain related to a weaker embarrassment reaction, we next examined the participants' brain scans. After looking at all potential brain regions, we found that the people who were the least reactive to watching themselves sing had the smallest volume in the right anterior cingulate cortex.[80] As we learned with Jaime, this part of the brain is important for producing emotions, and especially negative emotions like embarrassment. Although this study focused on people with the behavioral variant of FTD, these findings reflect a more general principle about the brain that applies to all of us. We differ in how easily we experience self-conscious emotions, and those of us who are prone to experiencing strong embarrassment may have a robust right anterior cingulate cortex. Clark had significant atrophy in this region. His embarrassment back-up system no longer worked, leaving him unremorseful and unapologetic.

People with the behavioral variant of FTD are not only less inclined to follow social rules, but many cross the line and break the law. Physicians Madeleine Liljegren and Georges Naasan found that nearly 40 percent of individuals with the behavioral variant of FTD exhibited criminal behavior in the early stages of their illness.[81] Their offenses were often silly, impulsive, and poorly planned. One person was arrested after he ate popsicles in a store and left without paying. Another trespassed on her neighbor's property despite being asked to stop. These individuals knew that what they were doing was wrong, but they could no longer control their impulses. This misbehavior was an early manifestation of their disease.

All things considered, Clark's changes in behavior suggested that he had the behavioral variant of FTD. During our meeting, Ellen and Clark had distinct reactions when I shared his diagnosis. Clark was quiet and did not ask any questions. Ellen cried quietly but soon composed herself. As is the case with many family members of people with FTD, she had already read enough to prepare herself for this news. She was as certain about his diagnosis as I was.

"Is there any cure, any treatment?" she asked.

I paused. "No, there are no cures yet. I think we should try an antidepressant. It might help with Clark's irritability and desire for alcohol.

I will put that recommendation in my note to your family physician. But I also want to focus on your health, Ellen. Are you able to get time away to relax?"

"Yes, I exercise regularly," Ellen sighed. "My children and friends are often with me. I will be OK." I could tell she was uncomfortable talking about her own health and that she wanted to move on, so I did. "Ellen, I admire you for your amazing fortitude and grace in the face of such a tough illness. It has not been easy, and you have done everything you can. And, Clark, I know that you are doing all that you can, too." They both nodded. When we said our goodbyes, Ellen seemed both relieved and disappointed. She felt relief because Clark finally had a diagnosis, and disappointment because she saw the daunting future ahead. It was not an uncommon reaction.

Over the course of the next few months, I worked with Clark's legal team as they prepared for his court appearance. Although the prosecutors would argue that his crimes were a midlife crisis worsened by alcohol, I was confident that there was a neurological explanation and believed FTD had led him to abuse alcohol in later life. Could he be held responsible for his actions if they were caused by a neurodegenerative disorder that increased his desire for rewards and decreased his ability to control his impulses? I did not think so. But the police and prosecutors thought otherwise. I also understood their perspective.

I sent Clark's lawyers my clinical note in which I detailed the results of his neurological and neuropsychological examinations as well as my diagnostic impressions. We discussed several strategies that they might use with the judge, but I was not asked to testify. In the end, Clark was sentenced to one year of probation and was spared from going to jail. He was also offered continued rehabilitation at a specialized center. In the end, it was a fair decision. On a phone call the following week, Ellen, Clark, and I discussed the outcome and our shared feelings of relief.

The frontal lobes are just beginning to receive attention in legal circles. We all vary enormously in how well our frontal lobes work, but where does personal responsibility end? Few people meet the criteria for legal insanity in criminal trials, and the M'Naghten rule is highly controversial. Existing laws, however, are hard to change. Could the legal system do more to consider a defendant's brain functioning when determining culpability? This is a challenging question that we must grapple with to make progress in our legal and medical communities. FTD is a powerful model for understanding frontal lobe disorders. Our research could help in the quest to update how we determine culpability in people with neurological or psychiatric conditions who break laws. Although there are still many complex issues to resolve in this area, the incorporation of principles from modern neuroscience into our legal systems may lead to better understanding and more rational sentencing.[82]

Clark would not have committed the crimes that he did if he did not have FTD. He lost his capacity to curb his desires and did not respect the rules of society. Like many people with the behavioral variant of FTD, Clark also no longer engaged in deep self-reflection to weigh the pros and cons of these actions. A lack of self-awareness is problematic for people with FTD, and for all of us, because we lose sight of who we are.

5 Self-Awareness

Humans rely on multiple sources of information to navigate their social environments. With our sense organs, we perceive the world around us. Signals from within our bodies, our "gut feelings," interact with these sensory data and shape our beliefs. Together, these streams of information not only help us to understand other people but also allow us to know who we are—to have a sense of "self."

Self-awareness is the ability to see ourselves in an accurate manner, that is, to see ourselves as others do. This is easier to achieve for some aspects of the self than others. To evaluate the physical self, we can look in a mirror to confirm that our appearance is as we imagined. We can touch our torso and limbs to determine whether they are where we think they are. With common tools, such as scales and stethoscopes, we can obtain objective measures about our bodies like our weight and heart rate.

There are other aspects of the self that are more subjective. Only we know the emotional landscape of our internal world, and we alone have privileged access to our thoughts and feelings. Emotions come and go but have a powerful influence both on how we see ourselves and how we see others. When we feel good, we may indulge in optimistic daydreams about future successes. When we feel down, we may doubt our prospects and assume the worst about ourselves and others. Whether we realize it or not, our ideas and emotions are intertwined and difficult, if not impossible, to separate. In extreme circumstances, our emotions can hijack rational thought and lead us to false conclusions about who we are.

Most of us have a keen sense of self. Our personalities and beliefs solidify in young adulthood and remain stable across our lifetimes. As adults we know who we are, but we are also able to imagine a range of other possibilities for who we could be. None of us is immune from thinking about how our lives could have turned out, or who we could have become, had we made different choices.[83] We can entertain these thoughts, but we can also dismiss ideas about ourselves that are untrue. It is one thing to imagine running a marathon or composing a symphony and another to believe one has achieved those things when one has not. We rely on fact-checking systems in the brain to prevent us from being dishonest with ourselves.

DOI: 10.4324/9781003502357-7

Emotions can hijack self-awareness by elevating certain ideas in our minds. While strong emotions may lead us to develop unlikely ideas about ourselves, we can usually ascertain the truth by considering the evidence. Self-reflection is an important safeguard that prevents us from accepting all our thoughts as facts. If we lose the ability to self-reflect, we may have difficulty sorting fact from fiction. People with disorders of the frontal lobes, such as those with the behavioral variant of FTD, have trouble assessing the plausibility of their ideas. Influenced by their emotions, they may abandon solid beliefs about who they are and embrace questionable or false new ideas. The story of Amit, a man with the behavioral variant of FTD, illustrates what happens when powerful emotions alter one's sense of self and disrupt self-awareness.

Dr. Miller's Clinical Note

Amit arrived at my office with his brother, Deepak. A tall man in his early fifties, Amit wore an old blue baseball cap that framed his face. His clothes were neat but casual—dark jeans, sneakers, and a gray sweatshirt—an outfit that seemed to signal wealth and power, Silicon Valley-style.

"Hello, Dr. Miller," Deepak said to me warmly as he extended his hand. "Thank you for fitting us into your busy schedule. I'm looking forward to hearing your thoughts about my brother, Amit."

"Hello, Deepak. It is nice to meet you," I replied, shaking his hand before turning to Amit. "And, Amit, it is also a pleasure to meet you."

Amit's face brightened when I addressed him. Smiling, he walked toward me and put his hand on my shoulder. "Bruce, I can't wait to tell you about my businesses. You will learn a lot!" Amit stated enthusiastically. He was standing much closer to me than was comfortable.

"I'm looking forward to it!" I said.

In a medical setting, greetings between doctors and patients usually maintain an air of formality. Such an informal greeting from a patient at a first visit is highly unusual. I began to make mental notes: Amit's use of my first name, his breech of my personal space, and his suggestion that he would teach me about business were important clues about what could be happening in his brain. Amit was correct in stating that I would learn a lot from him, but not in the ways that he thought.

"Have a seat. Tell me what brings you in," I continued.

"Life is great—I have no complaints. I don't know why I am here actually. Everything is the same as it's always been. In fact, it's better. I've never felt so good! I'm at the top of my game," Amit exclaimed.

Deepak pursed his lips, and his cheerful expression faded. "Dr. Miller, we are here because Amit has been diagnosed with the behavioral variant of FTD."

It may seem obvious that we know who we are from moment to moment, but self-awareness is a complex ability that is difficult to achieve. To possess self-awareness, there must be a close alignment between how we see ourselves and how others see us. The self is built from multiple interconnecting circuits that the brain tracks.[84] At the simplest level, the brain maps our body's boundary so that we know where our physical self begins and ends. As infants, we learn the difference between what is self and what is not. Self-awareness also includes knowing where we are and what we are doing. Infants gain control of their bodies as they learn to sit, crawl, and walk. In early childhood, the psychological elements of the self also begin to develop. We begin to prefer certain foods, toys, clothing, and people, and our likes and dislikes strengthen as we get older. As we gain life experiences, we develop beliefs about who we are. Our identity continues to mature during adolescence and stabilizes in early adulthood. Large swings in a healthy adult's personality, behavior, and beliefs are rare.

Only humans and a few other highly social species exhibit complex forms of self-awareness. Most creatures lack even basic self-awareness, such as the ability to recognize themselves in a mirror. Human infants take time to achieve this skill, which emerges in the second year of life. Babies with a smudge of rouge on their nose who are placed in front of a mirror will reach for the child in the mirror rather than their own nose.[85] As these infants cannot yet appreciate that they are the child in the mirror, they think that it is someone else with a strange mark on their face in front of them. After 18 months of age, they realize that it is their own reflection in the mirror and reach for their own nose instead (Figure 5.1). Some chimpanzees and orangutans can also pass similar tests of mirror self-recognition, and elephants and dolphins have a rudimentary capacity to perform this task as well.[86] Like humans, these species understand that they are the animal they see in the mirror, while most others do not.

Self-awareness also requires us to maintain an accurate understanding of our behaviors, emotions, and personality. This understanding forms the basis of how we see ourselves, and we experience intense feelings when others challenge our beliefs. According to neuroscientists Ethan Bromberg-Martin and Tali Sharot, it is the beliefs themselves that evoke rewarding feelings. These positive feelings prevent us from changing our opinions and jumping from one idea to another.[87] We are particularly reluctant to let go of beliefs with deep emotional significance and require substantial evidence to change our minds.

In people with FTD, their strong beliefs about who they are may fade away. As their sense of self becomes permeable, they show alterations in aspects of their identity that do not usually change in adulthood.[88] Some individuals suddenly convert to different religions while others switch political parties, modify their style of dress, or shift their culinary preferences. While these dramatic changes distress family members, the person with FTD often does not realize that they have changed. Sometimes, their emotions lead them to form beliefs about themselves that are not based in facts.

Figure 5.1 At 18 months of age, human infants begin to recognize themselves in the mirror.

"Deepak, can you please tell me about Amit's first symptoms?" I asked. Amit paced around the room as Deepak detailed the changes he had observed in his brother over the past few months.

For most of his career, Amit worked as a software developer at one of Silicon Valley's most successful companies. When Amit turned 50, his wife filed for divorce after several years of escalating conflict. She complained that Amit no longer cared about their relationship and that Amit had lost his love and compassion. Amit disagreed but was unmotivated to work through their issues. Although Amit seemed sad to others when his marriage ended, two months later, he was back to his cheerful self. The improvements in his mood did not stop there, and he was happier than he had ever been. Amit became elated.

Deepak next recounted a recent story that was particularly alarming to him. Amit had called Deepak at three in the morning, speaking at a feverish pitch. "I'm going to climb Mt. Tamalpais tonight. Do you want to join me? I want to leave soon!" Amit yelled into the phone. Deepak listened as Amit went on to describe in detail the various trails he planned to take. Unnerved by Amit's racing thoughts, boundless energy, and lack of awareness about the inconsiderate timing of his call, Deepak immediately drove to his brother's house to check on him. When Deepak arrived, he called out for Amit but got no response. Panicked, Deepak searched all the rooms of the house but could not find his brother. Noticing the outside lights on, Deepak went to the backyard where he found Amit painting the exterior wall of the house.

"The paint back here is peeling. I need to give this wall a quick coat!" Amit yelled over his shoulder, unfazed by his brother's sudden appearance.

"Right now?" Deepak retorted, stunned by his brother's behavior.

"Why not? It's the perfect time because it's not too hot. And it won't take long because I am so strong!" Amit said as he hastily moved the paint roller across the back wall.

"Amit, since when do you know how to paint houses?" Deepak queried, confused by Amit's responses.

"Are you crazy? I've always been an amazing house painter!" Amit replied with excitement.

Upon hearing Amit's reply, a wave of concern swept over Deepak. This was not the Amit he knew. Amit had always had a keen sense of who he was and was aware of his strengths and weaknesses. Amit's mood was not only elevated, but his ideas about himself and his accomplishments were untrue. Amit had never been grandiose before, and Deepak knew that he needed to seek medical advice for his brother.

The doctor who examined Amit soon after the house-painting incident diagnosed him with bipolar disorder. A telltale sign of bipolar disorder is mania. During manic episodes, people exhibit pressured speech, increased energy, sleeplessness, and irritability. They may also demonstrate heightened impulsivity and risk-taking behaviors. Some individuals with bipolar disorder swing between these bouts of euphoria and periods of low mood in which they experience symptoms of depression. Given that Amit displayed features of mania, bipolar disorder was a reasonable diagnosis at the time of his first evaluation. As his behavior continued to change over the next few months, however, his doctor wondered whether bipolar disorder was the correct diagnosis. She began to think that Amit might have the behavioral variant of FTD.

It can be very difficult for even experienced clinicians to distinguish between bipolar disorder and the behavioral variant of FTD. Unbridled positive emotions occur in both conditions and make these disorders challenging to disentangle. In our laboratory studies, we find people with FTD not only have strong positive reactions to videos and photographs that other people find cute or funny, but they also smile and laugh at objects and situations that others do not find amusing at all. Neutral images (photographs of sinks, power cords, and tables, for example) and even negative images evoke positive emotions in people with FTD.[89] Positive feelings in FTD are often indiscriminate. As neuropsychologist Ian Robertson notes, positive emotions boost our confidence and drive us to achieve.[90] Excessive positivity, however, can be maladaptive. To respond to life's many trials and tribulations, we need the ability to experience a range of feelings that includes positive as well as negative states. We cannot share in another's suffering without our own feelings of despair. Without negative feelings, we cannot respond to information that tells us to be cautious or suspicious. Self-awareness suffers when our confidence is too high, and we have an overly rosy view of ourselves that does not align with the evidence. Amit's soaring positivity led him to become grandiose and delusional. As he lost touch with reality, he lost the trust of people around him, and his decision-making deteriorated. He no longer saw himself as others did.

"Amit, your brother tells me you are good at painting houses. Is that true?" I asked.

"Why, yes! I have painted at least a hundred houses. I am also an excellent chef. I have a special salad dressing that I want to tell you about," Amit replied.

"A special salad dressing?" I asked. "That sounds interesting. Please tell me about it—is it something you make?" I was beginning to see that Amit not only tended to brag but that he also wildly exaggerated his own skills without considering how he might come across to others. He was blissfully unaware of the skepticism that others, including me, displayed when hearing his tall tales.

"I make the salad dressing at home. It is the world's best, and a lot of people want to buy it from me!" Amit responded. "How many people do you think?" I inquired, curious to hear his response.

"Five billion people want a bottle of this delicious stuff. I'm about to open a factory and hire thousands of workers who can mix the dressing to my exact specifications. I will be the king of salad dressing! Imagine, billions of people buying my special brand," Amit said, his eyes glistening with excitement.

Deepak quietly shook his head as he listened to his brother's claims, but Amit seemed oblivious to his reaction.

I turned to Deepak. "Is Amit this enthusiastic about other things in life, like spending time with friends and family?" Deepak lowered his gaze, and I did not need to hear his response.

"Amit, may I please check a few things?" I asked. He nodded, and I shined a small flashlight into each eye to see how they responded to the light. I instructed Amit to mimic a few different shapes that I made with my hands, and I watched how quickly he could tap his index finger and his thumb. I pulled a small rubber mallet from my bag and tapped his elbows and knees to measure his reflexes. I also observed him as he walked down the hallway. Amit did well on all these tests, which was not surprising given that he had no motor and sensory symptoms. From Deepak's story, it was clear that Amit had changed dramatically in recent years. While people with bipolar disorder can have an elevated mood and expansive beliefs like Amit, most individuals exhibit their first symptoms by their twenties. This was the first clue that bipolar disorder was an unlikely diagnosis as Amit did not have any trouble with mood until his fifties. I learned from my mentor, Dr. Benson, that when an adult exhibits significant changes in behavior, beliefs, or personality, it means that there has been a change in the brain. Dr. Benson also told me that people with frontal lobe disorders are prone to exaggerate and even lie because they are not worried about the negative impression they make on others. He called this "wild confabulation." Amit was certainly a wild confabulator! He told one implausible story after another.

As I looked at Amit's brain MRI, the most striking areas of atrophy were in the frontal lobes. The parts of the frontal lobes that were most affected were the dorsolateral prefrontal cortex and the medial prefrontal cortex. There is not usually this much atrophy in bipolar disorder, and I agreed with his previous doctor that bipolar disorder was unlikely to have caused the changes in Amit. Overall, his brain scan, as well as his symptoms, suggested that he had the behavioral variant of FTD.

Fueled by his strong positive emotions, Amit's exaggerated sense of his accomplishments led him to develop grandiose delusions. As the delusions that he formed gained traction in his mind, his self-awareness faded. While much is unknown about the brain systems that must go awry for delusions to emerge, prominent theories propose there must be at least "two hits." That means at least two different circuits must malfunction for delusions to take hold. While the first hit prompts the delusional beliefs to emerge, the second hit disrupts one's ability to evaluate whether the delusional beliefs are true.[91]

The site of the second hit in Amit was clear from his MRI. The most notable atrophy in Amit's scan was in the dorsolateral prefrontal cortex, a region that helps us to sift through various possible ideas. We have hypotheses about ourselves and the world, but when we obtain information that defies our expectations, this region helps us to reject inaccurate ideas and to update our beliefs.[92] Atrophy or dysfunction in the dorsolateral prefrontal cortex makes people less able to assess the plausibility of their ideas and to recognize when reliable data contradict their beliefs. Amit had no doubts that he was a great house painter and that his salad dressing would soon dominate the world's culinary scene. The pleasant feelings these beliefs elicited overrode his need to determine the truth. The version of himself that Amit had in his mind did not align with the facts, but he was oblivious.

If the dorsolateral prefrontal cortex was the second hit in Amit's brain, where was the first hit? Changes in emotions and mood, either positive or negative, can be the first hit that sets the stage for delusional thinking. It is likely that the origins of Amit's unrealistic beliefs can be traced to the circuits that produce and control positive emotions. Dysfunction in these systems drove Amit to become euphoric and fueled his grandiose ideas about his abilities and accomplishments.

In other individuals, the first hit might affect another brain circuit and cause different symptoms. If the first hit results in heightened negative emotions, people may experience severe depression and pessimistic ideas about themselves and others. They may develop self-deprecatory delusions and believe they are a bad person who is harmful to others or is cursed by the devil. Paranoia is common, and they may develop false beliefs that others are out to get them.

As I pondered the brain circuits responsible for Amit's grandiose delusions, I thought back to other people who had come to our clinic with delusional thinking. Lydia, a woman I had met years before, had a different type of delusion. Her story inspired me to think about the origins of false beliefs in the brain.

Lydia was 81 years old when she came to see me with Ron, her husband of 60 years. Lydia smiled and held Ron's hand throughout our meeting. She denied any difficulties with thinking and had no concerns about her capabilities. Ron had a different opinion which he did not vocalize here, but prior to our meeting, he had told me about a recent incident that caused him great distress.

Ron and Lydia had spent a leisurely afternoon together. After enjoying an early dinner and watching the evening news, Lydia retired to their bedroom. When Ron followed a few minutes later, Lydia shrieked, "Who are you? You look like Ron, but you are an impostor! You are not him. Get out of my house!" Before Ron could respond, Lydia dialed 911.

"Send the police—there is a trespasser in my house!" Lydia wailed into the phone. Stunned, Ron begged Lydia to believe that he was her husband. He had rarely seen her so upset and struggled to calm her down. He tried several strategies. First, he reminded her of the day they had just spent together. When that did not work, he gathered photo albums and showed her pictures of their wedding, children, and grandchildren. Despite Ron's efforts, Lydia remained suspicious and agitated. As I listened to Ron tell this story, I was impressed by how rational he had been while trying to persuade Lydia that he was really her husband. Unfortunately, Ron's pleas were ineffective.

When the police arrived, Lydia, who had been hiding in the closet, jumped out and continued to shout that Ron was not her husband. Believing that Lydia was in danger, the police handcuffed Ron. As he began to cry, it was as if a switch were flipped in Lydia. Her preserved empathy brought Lydia to her senses despite the irrational beliefs about Ron's identity.

Immediately, Lydia's wrath shifted from Ron to the police. "How dare you enter my house like this! Why are you doing this to my poor husband? Leave now!" Bewildered, the officers checked to make sure that Ron was truly Lydia's husband and then departed.

As we sat together in my office, Ron was hesitant to mention this incident to Lydia. He was afraid that she would become upset if he asked her about that evening. I, too, was unsure how she would respond to my inquiries, but I needed to hear her point of view. Ron and I agreed that I should go ahead and talk to Lydia about it.

"Lydia, Ron told me about a recent evening in which you had trouble recognizing him, and the police came to your house," I began. "Can you please tell me what happened?"

"I've never had trouble recognizing Ron—he's my husband!" she replied. Taken aback by her response, Ron looked at her and solemnly nodded in agreement. I sat quietly and asked no more questions but wondered what went wrong in Lydia's brain when she misidentified Ron on that mysterious evening.

In 1923, psychiatrist Joseph Capgras described the case of Madame M.[93] Like Lydia, Madame M. developed a delusion that an impostor had replaced her husband. For many years, her symptoms, which would later become known as "Capgras syndrome," were considered psychiatric in nature. Although people with Capgras syndrome believe that an impostor has replaced someone they know, other delusions of misidentification can involve animals or buildings. People with such delusions may think their cat is not their real cat or that their house is not their actual house. When these types of delusions emerge, people, pets, and places maintain a physical resemblance with the originals, but they have lost their emotional significance. What was once familiar is no longer so.

Delusions of misidentification arise in several psychiatric and neurological conditions. Individuals with schizophrenia or other forms of psychosis can develop this kind of delusion, as can people with certain neurodegenerative disorders. Dementia with Lewy bodies is a neurodegenerative disorder that has much in common with Parkinson's disease. In both disorders, people develop motor symptoms including reduced facial behavior, tremor, stiff muscles, shuffling gait, and stooped posture. Individuals with dementia with Lewy bodies also experience cognitive decline, and symptoms of anxiety and depression are common. Fluctuating levels of alertness as well as visual hallucinations are other hallmark features. The visual hallucinations often involve small living creatures such as insects, tiny animals, or even miniature people. Some individuals with dementia with Lewy bodies see shadowy figures out of the corner of their eye or feel a presence behind their shoulder.

At her next visit, Lydia told me that she saw tiny people and spiders invading her home at dusk. These visual hallucinations came and went and only bothered her for several minutes. Lydia continued to misidentify Ron on occasion, but these episodes were brief and lacked the emotional intensity of the first incident. Her alertness waxed and waned throughout the day. Her hallucinations and delusions tended to occur on evenings when she was fatigued.

In terms of her cognitive functioning, Lydia demonstrated some difficulties. She exhibited deficits in executive functioning and could no longer organize her grocery list or cook complex meals that required planning. Movement became more difficult as her muscles stiffened. When she sat quietly with her hands in her lap, her left hand trembled. Ron observed that Lydia's facial expressions were much more muted than they had been in the past.

Based on Lydia's symptoms, I diagnosed her with dementia with Lewy bodies. As with FTD, frontal lobe functioning declines in people with this condition. On a brain scan, however, the frontal lobes do not look as small in dementia with Lewy bodies as they do in FTD. This was true for Lydia, but her MRI revealed that she had subtle atrophy in the dorsolateral prefrontal cortex and medial prefrontal cortex.

Lydia and Amit shared the same second hit in the dorsolateral prefrontal cortex. As was true for Amit, loss of function in this region made it hard for Lydia to evaluate the feasibility of her beliefs. While Lydia was unable to assess how likely it was that a man in her home who resembled her husband was not really him, Amit could not determine how plausible it was that he was a skilled house painter with a priceless salad dressing. If Lydia and Amit could have taken a step back to assess the likelihood that their beliefs were true, they might have doubted their assertions or concluded that their ideas were illogical. Without an intact belief evaluation system, it was challenging for them to sort through competing possibilities about the world, leaving them open to accepting ideas not backed by facts (Figure 5.2).

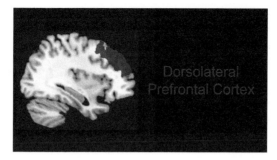

Figure 5.2 The dorsolateral prefrontal cortex helps us to evaluate the feasibility of our beliefs.

Lydia's delusions differed from Amit's, however, because she had a different first hit. Unlike Amit, whose increasing positives drove him to grandiose delusions, Lydia lost access to the cues that typically helped her to recognize Ron as her husband. Philosopher William Hirstein and neuroscientist V.S. Ramachandran have suggested that in Capgras syndrome, faces become disconnected from the emotional cues in the body that usually imbue known people with a glow of familiarity.[94] Without these internal signals, family members, friends, and acquaintances seem unfamiliar and are more easily rendered strangers—or even impostors. Although Lydia had known Ron for decades, his face no longer felt familiar to her in those fleeting moments in the evening when she was tired and inattentive.

When considering the reasons that Lydia and Amit developed delusions, it is possible that they had not just two, but three, hits to their brain circuitry. Neurologist Ryan Darby has found that people with delusions of misidentification also have dysfunction in medial networks that lie along the brain's

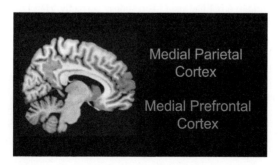

Figure 5.3 Medial prefrontal cortex and medial parietal cortex are midline structures that support self-reflection.

midline.[95] The medial prefrontal cortex has tight connections with the medial parietal cortex, and together this system allows us to create and recall the episodic memories of our lives (Figure 5.3). This is the circuit that we engage by default when we let our minds wander freely—be it when we are on a walk or jog or in the bath or shower—and this circuit activates as we think back on experiences from our lives and imagine the future.[96] By promoting self-reflection, the medial prefrontal cortex is important for self-awareness, but this system can go into overdrive when we ruminate about the effectiveness of our past words and actions. In Lydia, dysfunction in the medial prefrontal cortex may have made it difficult for her to recollect her decades of experiences with Ron and all the emotions those memories once carried. Without access to her memories and feelings, she was left to conclude that the person in front of her was not really the Ron that she knew. In Amit, dysfunction in the medial prefrontal cortex may also have left him unable to conjure up memories from his past that reminded him who he was. Without those memories to anchor his sense of self, Amit may have become open to see himself in new ways.

As I walked home from work after my meeting with Amit and Deepak, my mind wandered as it does after every busy day in the clinic. These moments of introspection often bring back a flood of ideas and feelings about the day as well as worries about the future. I thought back on the questions I had asked Amit and Deepak and wondered if I had forgotten to inquire about anything important. At one point in our conversation, Deepak pressed me for an opinion about the reasons for Amit's divorce. He wanted to know if the end of Amit's marriage was due to his emerging FTD. As I did not have firsthand knowledge of the events or detailed information about Amit's behavior during that time, I deferred an answer this question. While I thought Deepak understood my reasoning for not speculating about the reasons for the divorce, I now wondered if I had read his response correctly. Had I explained my thinking clearly? I hoped so.

As I contemplated my day, I also realized that Amit no longer engaged in this type of internal dialogue. Without the ability to self-reflect, he could not play back the events of his life and use that information to update his ideas about himself. Memories are the backbone of how we see ourselves and the labels and qualities that we feel best describe us. I know I am a neurologist, for example, because I can think back to my medical school, residency, and fellowship training, and I can recall many experiences with patients in the decades since. But without those memories, how would I see myself now? Would I know with certainty that I am a doctor if my memories were hazy or no longer personally meaningful? It is likely that I would be less certain about who I am if

I could not reminisce on past events and recall evidence that supported my assertions. If I had a weaker sense of my professional identity, perhaps I would even be open to suggestions about who I am. I might change how I see myself on a whim depending on my own emotional state.

Amit's self-awareness suffered because his ability to turn inward and to reflect on his emotions and actions had declined. He could no longer back up his claims about himself with facts but did not seem to mind. It also occurred to me that Amit might no longer know who he used to be. If he no longer knew the person he had been before his illness, how would he be able to know that he had changed?

The precision of our memories may fade over time, but our experiences form the basis of our beliefs about ourselves.[97] We know the traits that best describe us because we can remember events that support our views. If we think we are shy or outgoing, for instance, we can give examples from our lives to back up our opinions. Across our lifetimes, we build and refine our ideas about ourselves and the world, and we update our sense of self to incorporate current information. This flexibility allows us to maintain accurate self-awareness as we grow and change. In FTD, this malleability can go too far, and people no longer have insight into who they are. For Amit, his sense of self became porous as his self-reflection waned.

The facts that we know about ourselves are one form of semantic knowledge. Whereas episodic memories are personal memories of our life experiences, semantic knowledge refers to information we know that is not tied to a specific time or place.[98] As the facts that Amit knew about himself lost their connections to his episodic memories and emotions, even his most personal semantic knowledge degraded. Freed from the typical binds of a carefully constructed self, Amit was open to new ideas about who he was, and his emotions drove which possibilities gained prominence in his mind.

Semantic knowledge refers not only to information that we have accrued about ourselves but also to the facts that we know about the world around us. In other forms of FTD, people lose more general semantic knowledge and no longer understand what words mean or what objects do. Just as losing semantic knowledge about oneself can open new possibilities—allowing a person to make drastic changes in how they behave and what they believe—losing semantic knowledge of other concepts can also be freeing in unexpected ways.

6 Openness

Just as we must maintain stability and flexibility in our sense of self, we must also strike a balance between openness and knowledge. Being open not only enables us to solve everyday problems but also allows us to have experiences that we did not anticipate. When we keep an open mind in social interactions, we may often discover that we have things in common even with people who at first seem quite different from us.[99] While openness opens doors to innovative ideas, our knowledge also influences how we see the world and is critical for creativity.

Semantic knowledge refers to the facts that we have learned about ourselves and the world through our life experiences. Although formal education is important for learning, day-to-day exposure to different people, cultures, and ideas also deepens our semantic knowledge. Throughout our lives, we develop detailed semantic knowledge about many things. Some types of semantic knowledge pertain to words and objects. We all know about various kinds of tools and birds, but some of us know more than others and have more refined semantic knowledge about these areas. Other kinds of semantic knowledge center on social information. We learn what emotions look and feel like, and we acquire facts and opinions about people. As our semantic knowledge becomes more complex through learning and experience, specific circuits in the social brain become increasingly elaborate and connected with other parts of the brain.

Semantic knowledge yields many benefits. We are better teachers, advisors, conversationalists, and troubleshooters when we have expertise in select domains of semantic knowledge. Knowing facts about various areas may foster openness by allowing people to forge connections between ideas that are usually unlinked.[100] Finding these commonalities between disparate topics can enable people to think outside the box and, in some cases, to break from traditional ways of seeing and doing things.[101] Being open allows chefs to create new dishes with unexpected elements (corn is delicious on pizza, who knew?), musicians to craft unusual pieces and lyrics, and architects to design unconventional buildings. The possibilities are endless.

Although building semantic knowledge has its advantages and is an essential part of wisdom, in some cases our thinking is more flexible before our ideas about the world have cemented.[102] Imagination and curiosity abound in

DOI: 10.4324/9781003502357-8

early life as children have not yet learned where the boundaries are typically drawn between semantic categories and what is impossible. Young people are especially open to novel ideas because they are still searching for information about themselves and the world, and the boundaries between semantic categories are still porous. Adults know that pumpkins are not blue, cats do not have wings, and cars do not have triangular tires, but we can imagine them that way if we loosen the associations in our minds and make room for new possibilities. Remaining open to new experiences is critical as we age, but many people lose openness and become set in their ways as they get older. They may believe they know all there is to know about a topic or that they hold the best solution to every problem. If we develop rigid rules in our minds about how things are or how they should be, we may stifle new ways of thinking.[103]

In some older adults, openness does not wither but instead blossoms. We have discovered that when a neurodegenerative disorder causes a selective decline in semantic knowledge, people begin to connect ideas in ways that defy conventional ways of thinking. Such was the remarkable case of Markus. Although never interested in art earlier in life, Markus began to see the world in new ways as his semantic knowledge dissipated. The changes in his brain opened his mind to different ideas and motivated him to produce inspiring artistic creations.

Dr. Miller's Clinical Note

As I looked out into the waiting room, Markus was hard to miss in his purple pants and yellow shirt. A tall, thin man with curly gray hair, Markus's bright clothing stood in stark contrast to his reserved demeanor. When I greeted him, he responded, but his face was unexpressive. He was accompanied by his son, James. After a brief round of introductions, they followed me quietly down the hall to the small examination room where we would meet. James gave me a quick summary about why they had made an appointment with me.

Two months prior, James brought Markus to see their family physician because he had noticed changes in his father's mood and behavior. Markus had become quiet, and he was disinterested in spending time with his family and friends. His style of dress and interests had also shifted in notable ways. After hearing James describe these changes in Markus, their doctor diagnosed him with schizophrenia. James was not convinced this diagnosis was correct, however, and reached out to me a few weeks later for a second opinion.

"What is the most significant change that you have observed in your father, James?" I asked.

James retrieved a stack of Polaroids from his tote bag and placed them on my desk. The photographs showed a series of paintings, each striking for their play with colors and forms. One depicted a beautiful orange and yellow flower, its petals carefully crafted. Another focused on a sailboat that was unlike any I had ever seen. The sailboat featured a vibrant purple mast and a yellow sail—hues like those in Markus's outfit. The sail was not only part of the boat but also merged with the distant shore—it was both foreground and background (Figure 6.1). The painting was stunning and broke conventional rules about what a sailboat is.

"This is a beautiful painting. Your father is quite an artist," I remarked. Markus did not react to my comment but silently stared out the window.

"My father is not an artist. He was never interested in art." James said, without turning to look at me. "He is not the same person he used to be. I know his work is good, but he is not right. There is something different about him."

Figure 6.1 Example of a painting drawn in the style of Markus's sailboat painting. Illustration by Caroline Prioleau.

Traditionally, neurology is a discipline focused on loss. When first meeting a patient, the primary job of the neurologist is to determine if there is a problem in the nervous system. If there is a neurological deficit, the next question is which part of the nervous system is affected. After isolating the problem, the neurologist then tries to determine its cause. Until Oliver Sacks wrote about talent in people with neurological conditions, neurologists rarely inquired about the emergence of unexpected new skills.[104] New talents, like Markus's ability to paint, were considered irrelevant to the clinical evaluation. Dr. Sacks's approach to neurology inspired many others, including us, to explore more than just deficits. Our research has helped to define the strengths that can emerge in various neurological conditions. Still, the idea that there can be spared, or even enhanced, abilities in the context of devastating illnesses remains underappreciated and understudied.

"Can you tell me about your paintings?" I asked Markus. This was the first time I had ever asked a person in my clinic about a newly acquired skill. Eyes wide, I looked at him, eager to hear his response. Markus appeared indifferent to my question. "Paintings--what are paintings? I paint," he eventually responded.

It took me a minute to take in exactly what Markus had said. On the one hand, he did not seem to understand the word "painting." On the other hand, he answered my question using that same word in a different form. I realized that Markus could not understand the word "paint" when I used it as a noun in "painting," but he understood this same word when it was used as a verb. He himself had said, "I paint." I decided to try my question again, this time using "paint" as a verb.

"Why do you paint?" I asked.

"Let's go. Let's go. I paint colors. I feel colors," he said.

"Markus, tell me about the purple and yellow colors that you use in your work," I asked, trying unsuccessfully to make eye contact. I wondered whether he had chosen those colors intentionally or if he had selected them without realizing it. I was not sure that he would know.

"I feel purple. I feel yellow... I want to go," Markus replied while staring at the floor. He was eager to make a quick exit.

When James had asked his father about his new preoccupation, Markus did not offer any reasons for painting. Unlike many artists, Markus had little interest in communicating with others through his work, and it was nearly impossible to engage him in even brief discussions about his paintings. His main goal seemed to be satisfying an unrelenting drive to paint. The interest that Markus had in painting did not begin with a pace that is typical of a new midlife hobby but rather took hold of him suddenly. Painting soon consumed most of his waking hours. Markus's first pieces were simple lines—scribbles primarily, sometimes dots—that he made with crayons. Soon, he turned to watercolors and painted crude pictures of apples and peaches or the models who posed in his art class. His watercolors were mesmerizing, and their beauty was not due to luck or chance.

Markus had real talent, but the approach he took to his art was unusual. He repainted the same piece for weeks, or even months, and his insistence on getting each picture right helped him to perfect his technique. When he became obsessed with animals, he painted arrays of dogs, leopards, turtles, fish, and birds. It was during this period that he produced his most impactful art. Stacks of canvases quickly amassed in his basement as he painted for many hours every day. Within just a few years, Markus created hundreds, perhaps thousands, of paintings. Others soon took notice of his work. His pieces won prizes at several local art fairs, even beating the work of established artists with formal training who had painted for many years.

From the start of his artistic journey, Markus used colors in daring but somewhat predictable ways. It was clear from his paintings and his clothing that he preferred two colors, purple and yellow. Purple and yellow lie on opposite sides of the color wheel, and their juxtaposition creates a bold visual effect. Perhaps purple and yellow belong together, fused in our brains through an unknown neural process. Not surprisingly, these colors coexist in some of the most famous paintings in history such as "Starry Night" by Vincent van Gogh. These colors are also the centerpiece of many powerful songs. While "Yellow" by Coldplay is a love song that uses beautiful yellow images to convey feelings of warmth, "Purple Rain" by Prince describes the pain that arises when a relationship with a loved one ends. This is what great artists do—they use colors, images, stories, and sounds to invigorate our emotions.

Changes in Markus's brain altered his experience of purple and yellow. We perceive colors in the medial area of the occipital cortex at the very back of the brain, and an injury to this area would have made Markus unable to see colors. Colors did not fade away for him but instead gained vibrancy, and the regions of his brain that process colors seemed hyperactive. Markus saw colors intensely, and he also seemed to feel them, physically. Most of us cannot feel colors because separate pathways in the brain process the sensations of vision, touch, smell, taste, and hearing. In some individuals, two or more sensations become linked, a phenomenon called "synesthesia." Although rare, people with synesthesia hear colors, taste shapes, or feel sounds, experiences that neuroscientist V.S. Ramachandran has described in detail.[105] In synesthesia, neurons involved with two sensory modalities fire simultaneously, causing cross-associations between senses that people usually experience independently. Most individuals with synesthesia are born with the condition, having inherited a distinct brain organization, but others may experience synesthesia for other reasons.

Psychedelic drugs like lysergic acid diethylamide (LSD), peyote, ayahuasca, and psilocybin can cause synesthesia as well as visual hallucinations. Users of these substances may see flashing colors, beams of light, and halos. Often, these visions are purple or yellow in hue. (Many believe Jimi Hendrix's "Purple Haze" references both the color of a specific type of LSD tablet and the dense purple hallucinations that result from the drug.) They may also feel in their bodies the colors that they see. As James confirmed that Markus did not use drugs, it seemed unlikely that a substance was causing him to have synesthesia. Something else must have led Markus to fixate on purple and yellow. Was he hallucinating?

Hallucinations also arise in certain psychiatric disorders. In schizophrenia, people can hallucinate and develop delusions, lack of motivation, disorganized speech, trouble thinking, and compulsive behaviors. Although it is very rare for schizophrenia to emerge for the first time in late life, Markus had been diagnosed with this condition because he exhibited several of these symptoms. The hallucinations that occur in schizophrenia, however, are usually auditory, rather than visual, in nature. That is, people with schizophrenia are more likely to hear voices of people who are not there than they are to see things that others do not see. Markus's older age and symptom profile made it unlikely that he had schizophrenia. It was therefore doubtful that his interest in purple and yellow resulted from hallucinations.

In retrospect, James first noticed changes in his father six years earlier when his mother, Markus's wife of 40 years, passed away. Markus had worked in banking and was known for his strong work ethic. Quick to connect with clients and peers, Markus had always been gregarious and well liked. He had long been admired for the ease with which he navigated complex financial negotiations. After his wife's death, Markus's passion for banking waned. He soon retired. At first, James thought his father was depressed and still grieving, but then he noticed other changes.

Although Markus had more time on his hands, he withdrew from his friends and family. He seemed disengaged during social interactions and spoke little. His silence was unsettling. When Markus did speak, he had trouble finding words and would often use the wrong word. He said "dog" when he meant "cat" and "hat" when he meant "sweater," among other mix-ups. One time, he even called a cockroach a baby. Sometimes, Markus responded to questions with answers that did not entirely make sense, and James wondered if he had trouble comprehending what others were saying to him. James thought Markus had more difficulty understanding topics that were especially complex or abstract. When people begin to have trouble speaking or understanding words, it suggests there may be changes in the brain's language systems in the left side of the brain. This was indeed the case for Markus.

"What is this?" I asked Markus, showing him a picture of a parrot from a book of drawings that I carried with me for language testing. Markus furrowed his eyebrows as he stared at the page.

"That's a thing. An animal, maybe an animal," Markus replied. When I told him it was a parrot, he looked at me quizzically and responded, "Parrot? What is a parrot?"

To recognize a parrot, we must search through our libraries of semantic knowledge to find its name. The word "parrot" is connected to all the facts and experiences that we have with parrots as well as other birds and animals. Markus had no trouble repeating "parrot" after I had said the word, but his lack of semantic knowledge about parrots astounded me. He had just made a beautiful painting of a purple and yellow parrot—it was one of his masterpieces—but he did not know what a parrot was.

I turned the page to the next drawing in the book. We had a similar exchange when I showed him a picture of a hummingbird. When he could not identify the bird, I said, "This is a hummingbird."

"Hummingbird, hummingbird, what is a hummingbird? Does it hum?" Markus replied. I smiled encouragingly, again noting that he appeared more familiar with verb "hum" than with the noun "hummingbird."

Markus's questions reminded me of a woman, Rose, whom I had met years ago during my behavioral neurology fellowship with Dr. Benson. Rose had an unusual language disorder. She had lost her knowledge of the meaning of words, especially nouns. I recalled how Dr. Benson examined Rose's language abilities to isolate her specific areas of weakness.

"What are these?" Dr. Benson asked after extracting his keys from his pocket. He turned them around to show her all angles and shook them gently so that they jingled. Rose looked puzzled.

"You use them to open a door," he hinted. She continued to stare at him blankly. Dr. Benson handed Rose the keys, and she felt their metal edges with her fingers. She said nothing.

"Are these keys?" Dr. Benson probed, this time more directly.

"Keys... Keys... What are keys?" she asked.

Rose spoke with ease and had no trouble producing clear speech, but her semantic knowledge of words and objects was impaired. For most people, the sight, sound, and feel of the keys would have quickly helped them to remember their name. These cues did not help Rose. When Dr. Benson provided Rose with a clue about their function, and even their actual name, she still did not know what keys were. Rose had not only lost the word "key," but she had lost the entire concept of what a "key" was. Dr. Benson taught me that Rose had a specific type of aphasia--a disorder of speech or language. People with this rare type of aphasia lose semantic knowledge and no longer know what words and objects are. I wondered if Markus had the same type of aphasia that I had seen in Rose so many years before.

Speech and language rely on brain regions located in the left hemisphere.[106] Language has many functions, but none is more important than allowing us to communicate with others. When there is dysfunction in these systems due to a stroke, tumor, or head injury, a person may develop aphasia. There are many types of aphasia, and the symptoms of each type reflect loss of function in a specific part of the brain's speech and language system. In the 19th century, neuropsychiatrist Carl Wernicke described people with aphasia due to stroke in the posterior part of the temporal lobe.[107] Speech in these individuals remained fluent, and their words flowed without effort. Their comprehension was poor, however, and they did not realize that their sentences were jumbled and sometimes nonsensical.

Aphasia can also arise in the setting of neurodegenerative disorders. Neurologist Marsel Mesulam coined the term "primary progressive aphasia" to refer to speech and language problems that are caused by neurodegenerative disorders.[108] People with primary progressive aphasia have difficulty with speech or language that worsens over time. Eventually, they may have trouble in other areas of cognition and develop problems with behavior and movement. Like the individuals Wernicke described, Markus had fluent speech. Yet, because his comprehension and repetition were good, he did not meet criteria for a Wernicke-type aphasia. The problem that Markus had was different. He no longer understood the meaning of single words, a deficit that pointed to selective decline in semantic knowledge.

Semantic knowledge is comprised of layers of concepts that we acquire across our lifetimes. Like the levels in a pyramid, each layer of semantic knowledge is smaller and more refined than the one beneath it. We begin developing our semantic knowledge early in life and continue to deepen our understanding of different topics through education and experience. The more refined our semantic knowledge, the more levels we have in that concept's pyramid. As children, we form the base of our pyramids by acquiring broad concepts. When we first learn about animals, we understand that they are living creatures that eat, sleep, and breathe much like we do, but we do not know much about the distinct types. As we get older, we build on this basic infrastructure by learning about the various kinds of animals and their unique characteristics.

Over time, our semantic knowledge becomes more elaborate. We can not only differentiate among birds, reptiles, amphibians, and mammals, but we also know about the different types of animals in each of these categories. We begin to distinguish a "parrot"—a large-beaked, brightly colored bird from the tropics that can repeat phrases—from a "hummingbird"—a tiny bird that buzzes from flower to flower at dizzying speeds. People who are keen observers of birds accrue even more detailed information about each type of bird. They may know the size, coloring, beak shape, flight behavior, and song of different birds, and they can tell even commonly confused birds apart. Although a novice birdwatcher may not be able to distinguish between a house finch and a purple finch, a sophisticated birder knows that a house finch is noisier than a purple finch and has a slimmer head and streaks on its belly. Using all their senses, the birder with greater semantic knowledge can easily tell the difference between these very similar types of animals.

Each pyramid of semantic knowledge is built from many kinds of information. We associate words with concepts, and part of our semantic knowledge is comprised of information about the words themselves. We know what each word sounds like, how many syllables it has, and how it is spelled. We can picture what the word looks like when it is written in different ways—in cursive on a chalkboard, in our own handwriting in a notebook, or in block letters on a traffic sign. By referencing concepts, words allow us to communicate with others. The more nuanced our semantic knowledge, the better we can use words with precision to articulate our ideas and opinions. Semantic knowledge is more than just facts, however. Our feelings and memories imbue concepts with emotional significance.

Decades before other doctors realized that people with aphasia could exhibit selective loss of semantic knowledge, Dr. Benson was able to recognize people with this problem in his clinic. Dr. Benson had learned about this type of aphasia from his mentor, Norman Geschwind, one of the founders of behavioral neurology. In the 1970s, Dr. Geschwind described a form of aphasia in which people lose semantic knowledge.[109] He noted that people with this type of aphasia lose their understanding of words and concepts—especially nouns. Now known as the "semantic variant" of primary progressive aphasia, many researchers including John Hodges, Karalyn Patterson, Elizabeth Warrington, David Neary, Julie Snowden, and Maria Luisa Gorno Tempini have since defined the specific features of this syndrome.[110]

In the semantic variant of primary progressive aphasia, entire concepts gradually disintegrate. People with this type of aphasia first lose details of specific concepts that lie at the top of their semantic knowledge pyramid.[111] Without facts and memories of what makes a hawk a hawk, they can no longer appreciate how a hawk differs from a condor or a sparrow. Eventually, the

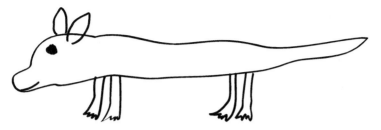

Figure 6.2 A drawing of snake that is like those made by people with the semantic variant of primary progressive aphasia.

boundaries between more disparate concepts become blurry. At this point, they might no longer see how hawks, or any birds for that matter, differ from reptiles, amphibians, or mammals. As each species continues to lose its distinguishing features, all animals are reduced to a common prototype. Hawks, dogs, and turtles become similar renditions of a generic animal concept that remains in their brains (Figure 6.2).

James found it difficult to pinpoint exactly when Markus's language troubles began, but he was certain that his father's symptoms were slowly progressing. At first, Markus mixed up similar words and referred to a bluejay as a "crow." As time went on, his errors were more dramatic. He would sometimes call a bird a "cat" or a "snake."

James brought a copy of Markus's brain MRI, which was completed three months earlier. If Markus had a neurodegenerative disorder, there would be notable loss of tissue in specific parts of his brain. Dr. Benson had taught me that people with the type of aphasia that disrupts semantic knowledge often have atrophy in the anterior regions of the brain—usually in the anterior temporal lobes. From the MRI, I could see that most areas of Markus's brain looked healthy. The frontal, parietal, and occipital lobes were plump and without any apparent changes. The left anterior temporal lobe, however, drew my attention as it was notably small. This region in the right was also smaller than it should have been.

The profound atrophy in Markus's brain ruled out schizophrenia and confirmed my suspicions that he suffered from a neurodegenerative disorder. The prominent atrophy in the anterior temporal lobes suggested that he had the semantic variant of primary progressive aphasia. As Markus's earliest symptoms reflected decline in his semantic knowledge of words and objects, I suspected that his disease began in the left anterior temporal lobe but, over time, had spread to the right.

The anterior temporal lobes are key regions in the social brain that represent semantic knowledge.[112] The more we know about concepts such as keys and hawks, the more plentiful and dense are the connections between the anterior temporal lobes and other brain regions. The anterior temporal lobes weave the tapestry of our semantic knowledge by binding words to images, sounds, movements, feelings, and tastes (Figure 6.3).

Both the left and right anterior temporal lobes are critical for semantic knowledge, but each has a different specialization. Whereas the left anterior temporal lobe is especially important for verbal semantic knowledge regarding words and objects, the right anterior temporal lobe plays a dominant role in nonverbal semantic knowledge centered on people and emotions.[113] We recognize familiar people because we know what they look like and how we feel about them. Our emotions help us to gauge how much we like, respect, or admire those around us and how much we want to spend time with them— or keep our distance. Just like we expand our semantic knowledge of other concepts throughout our lives, we continue to learn about our emotions as we age. Cultural influences and life experiences shape how we understand and articulate our feelings and how much we use our inner states to guide our decisions.

In the semantic variant of primary progressive aphasia, there is selective dysfunction in the anterior temporal lobes. For Markus, it is likely that the disease began in the left anterior temporal lobe and degraded his knowledge of words and their meanings. He no longer knew what objects were, and he had trouble comprehending single words because his verbal semantic knowledge had faded. Markus, like Rose, lost entire semantic concepts. Giving Rose clues about what keys do and letting her see and touch them did not help her to retrieve the name because she no longer knew what a key was. Markus had a similar problem. As the atrophy progressed to the right anterior temporal lobe, Markus lost his semantic knowledge of people and emotions. He was unable to comprehend his own emotions, and he lacked words to

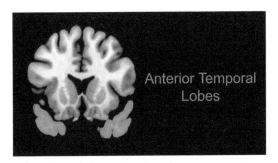

Figure 6.3 The left and right anterior temporal lobes.

express his feelings. Eventual dysfunction in the right anterior temporal lobe caused Markus, like Thomas, to lose empathy. Markus either failed to notice or was unable to recognize James's emotions, which made it difficult for him to respond in caring ways. While loss of empathy followed decline in semantic knowledge for Markus, Thomas showed the opposite pattern. In Thomas, severe atrophy in the right anterior temporal lobe disrupted empathy early in his disease. Although he may have had mild deficits in semantic knowledge, as evidenced by his difficulty naming uncommon objects on testing, this was not a prominent early symptom.

Markus lost his ability to understand language and people, but his declining semantic knowledge opened a world of possibilities for him in his art. Unconstrained by preconceived concepts of what animals, people, and emotions look like, Markus was free to craft his own versions. By painting animals in unconventional colors—purple and yellow birds, purple and yellow turtles, purple and yellow fish—he produced a world of whimsical creatures from his own imagination. As his semantic knowledge of animals receded, the details that once separated them faded, melding the animals in his mind into new fantastical combinations.

While many of the animals and humans that Markus painted lacked emotions entirely, others had curious blends. Markus's fading understanding of how faces typically display feelings allowed him to combine emotions in surprising ways. In one piece, he painted a beagle with a gaping mouth, which suggested joy, and flattened ears, which suggested anger. He formed new associations that were sometimes jarring. Although Markus may not have intended to communicate deeper messages to his audiences with his paintings, his unorthodox pieces evoked reactions of surprise and intrigue in those who viewed them. His new ways of seeing the world were unusual but added drama and allure to his paintings.

In the photographs James showed me, I noticed Markus's more recent paintings were increasingly abstract. His animals lost their specificity—his birds looked like fish, his dogs looked like birds or insects, and his turtles looked like snakes. The animals were haunting. Some of his paintings included unrecognizable creatures that had legs, a tail, and a block-shaped face. In these pieces, Markus's creations merged the features of many animals.

In one series, Markus painted large purple and yellow heads, floating in space and devoid of a body. A particularly arresting piece featured an upside-down head that protruded from the neck of a head that was right-side up. Both heads were expressionless. I inquired about this painting to see if Markus could explain what it meant.

"Are the heads connected for a reason? Is that your head?" I asked Markus, pointing at a photograph of the painting.

"No, they are purple and yellow."

"Are they sad? Markus, I wonder if you are sad when you paint?" I asked.

"What is sad?" he replied.

Unfortunately, my questions did not uncover the answers I was seeking. Conversations with Markus never provided insights into his motivation. I instead needed to rely on James's opinions and my own observations.

As the meaning of words slipped away, Markus lived in an increasingly nonverbal world. Without semantic knowledge, he had fewer assumptions about what he saw and heard. Humans rely enormously on vision to navigate the environment, and as Markus's semantic knowledge declined, his visual input became more powerful. He developed an acute visual awareness and saw even subtle changes and incongruities in the environment. Aside from painting, his favorite activity was walking the streets of his town looking for coins. Markus accumulated an enormous collection of pennies, nickels, dimes, and quarters that he kept from these excursions. "I never see a coin before he does," James remarked. Research by neuroscientist Indre Viskontas has shown that people with the semantic variant of primary of progressive aphasia approach visual pursuits with unique strategies and are able to see intricate details that might be missed by healthy individuals.[114]

For Markus, having an aphasia due to dysfunction in left hemisphere language circuits allowed new areas of his brain to flourish. A new visual fascination and a desire to paint were the first signs of his brain disease. Yes, his openness to new ideas and hobbies was the first sign of neurodegenerative disorder! His loss of semantic knowledge, though tragic, brought newfound abilities that allowed him to create stunning paintings in an exuberant style that was all his own. He began to see and experience the visual world with more fervor, and he formed associations between concepts that others had not. Markus approached objects with a new perspective, as if he had never seen them before, and he imagined new uses for them. What does one do with water if one no longer knows what water is? What could one do with scissors with no preconceived notions of what they are for? As Markus lost his semantic knowledge, even the human body lost its standard form, which led him to reorganize it as he pleased. An upside-down second head can attach to a neck in a world not limited by standard semantic associations. Markus was unique, but losses and gains are the story of neurodegenerative disorders. When there is decline in one region, other areas step in to help—this is no accident or coincidence but rather reflects the organization of the brain. While degeneration in the left anterior temporal lobe, a key region in the social brain, prompted Markus to paint, how other parts of his brain had changed in response to his disease was unknown.

Some of us are more open to new ways of thinking than others, but we all have room for creative growth. While artists more easily create paintings, music, dance, and stories than many of us, we all have the potential to deepen our openness and creativity. Artists, like other creative individuals, are often at the forefront of discovery and innovation because they stay open to new possibilities and see new things that others do not. In fact, the very idea that semantic knowledge could deteriorate in a person's brain did not first come from Dr. Geschwind, Dr. Benson, or any other brilliant scientist, but instead arose from the mind of one of the world's greatest writers. In *One Hundred Years of Solitude*, Gabriel García Márquez described a neurological illness that took over the tiny jungle town of Macondo and caused its victims to lose "the name and the notion of things."[115] To preserve their semantic knowledge, the people in Macondo recorded the names and uses of objects with the hope that this written information would guide them as their disease worsened. But just like people with the semantic variant of primary progressive aphasia, the citizens of Macondo continued to lose their understanding of words despite their efforts to prevent further decline.

Mr. Márquez published his classic novel in 1967, years before the neurological community ever knew there was a type of aphasia that could disrupt semantic knowledge. Did Márquez ever see a person with this uncommon type of aphasia? Possibly. Or did his well-known struggles with writer's block lead him to conjure up this condition from his own mind? The world will never know as, sadly, he himself developed dementia and did not have the opportunity to explain his uncanny ability to capture this neurological condition. Regardless of exactly how Mr. Márquez came to describe this unusual disorder of language, his openness to new possibilities propelled his creativity and storytelling to new heights. He used his keen powers of observation and imagination to craft a tale that continues to enthrall generations of readers.

Markus motivated new efforts to understand the systems in the social brain that make us open to new ideas. While creativity is widely admired, much remains unknown about the brain processes that allow us to think in unexpected ways. Only later did we learn how changes in Markus's social brain encouraged his brief but brilliant artistic career.

7 Creativity

The drive to create is a defining characteristic of the human species. Creativity has many dimensions but is rooted in the ability to connect ideas in a novel and compelling manner. Novel technologies, books, science experiments, exercise programs, dances, paintings, sculptures, architectural feats, recipes, movies, spiritual practices, and religious traditions are all born from human innovation. By integrating information in an unexpected and original manner, creative people can break from conventional ways of thinking and push the limits of human achievement.[116] We all have the capacity to generate new approaches to the problems that we face, but exceptional creativity is more than fixing the issues that we encounter in our daily lives. Rather, this requires *discovering* new ideas or creating new products that were previously unachievable.[117]

Creative thinking drives exceptional accomplishments but also permeates everyday life in less spectacular ways.[118] Creativity can appear in many settings—a creative plumber might find an innovative solution to a leaky pipe, and a creative taxi driver might take an unconventional route to avoid a traffic jam—but creativity truly takes center stage in the arts. Renowned comedians, such as Robin Williams, Mindy Kaling, and Kristen Wiig, do impressions and tell riotously funny stories that enlighten us about our humanity. Actors captivate our imaginations on the big screen. Only people with exceptional talent, such as James Earl Jones, Meryl Streep, and Bruce Willis, bring their characters to life with such acuity that others can hardly believe they are not actually the person they are portraying. Musicians like Bob Dylan, Carlos Santana, and Taylor Swift write and perform songs that move and inspire generations. By evoking strong emotions and allowing us to explore our common bonds, artists enrich our lives and offer novel insights about the world. Powerful songs, paintings, movies, and books not only can bring us joy and entertainment but can also change our perspectives by making us think in new ways.

We are born with different creative interests and abilities, but the brain circuits that help us to think in unexpected ways are modifiable. For some, the sound, spelling, and meaning of words are fascinating and may lead them to compose stories or poems. For others, colors, patterns, textures, and

DOI: 10.4324/9781003502357-9

shapes may inspire them to paint or sculpt. And for those who appreciate tone, melody, and rhythm, it may be that music, songwriting, or dance are the most alluring forms of expression. It is possible to shape our creativity in these areas by cultivating artistic skills or engaging in activities that encourage new ways of seeing the world. Sometimes, these shifts occur without conscious effort. As we saw with Markus, some people with neurodegenerative disorders have changes in the social brain that allow creativity to blossom. One way that visual creativity can emerge is when language circuits weaken. If visual information bombards your sensory experiences, as it did for Markus, one may feel compelled to depict that world through painting or other visual means.

Markus's story prompted us to investigate unresolved questions about the neuroscience of openness and creativity. These studies helped to elucidate how changes in the social brain relate to visual creativity but left many questions unanswered. Markus's artistic abilities flourished as his language networks declined, but it was not clear how this had happened. It was not until years later, when Anne and Robert Adams visited our center, that we began to understand how brain circuits in neurodegenerative disorders can reorganize and motivate people to create.

Dr. Miller's Clinical Note

Anne and Robert Adams traveled from their home in Vancouver, British Columbia to see me for an appointment in San Francisco. Anne was a biologist who specialized in the structure of intestinal cells, and Robert was a professor of mathematics. As a couple, they were devoted to each other, to their family, and to science.

"I hope you had a smooth flight down to San Francisco. How has your trip been so far, Anne?" I asked.

"Good," Anne said after a pause. I asked a few more questions, and she continued to respond slowly with one-word answers. Robert told me that for the past three years, Anne increasingly struggled to talk. Robert told me that, in recent months, she rarely spoke at all unless answering a direct question. During the rest of our meeting, Anne was silent.

To better understand Anne's symptoms, I invited neurologists Maria Luisa Gorno Tempini, Brandy Matthews, and William Seeley to evaluate her with me. Each member of our team brought a distinct perspective and helped me to understand the changes that were occurring in Anne. First, we assessed Anne's language abilities using standard tests. Sitting across from Anne at a narrow table, Dr. Gorno Tempini showed her a large white card. On the card was a complex line drawing that featured adults picnicking on a large grassy field.

"I'd like you to look at this picture," Dr. Gorno Tempini said slowly, articulating her words with care to facilitate understanding. "Please take your time and tell me what you see. And if you can, please try to speak in sentences."

Anne sat with her elbows propped on the table, her hands clasped together under her chin. She looked intently at the drawing on the card. "Tree," Anne said after a long silence. "Um, people," she said after another long pause. "Um," she added with a deep sigh, touching her forehead with her hand. "Dog," she added 15 seconds later. "Man," she said, pointing to the drawing.

While looking at the card, Anne exerted significant effort to produce just a few words over several minutes. To determine whether written expression was easier, we asked her to write a sentence. This, too, proved difficult. Anne's writing, like her verbal output, was laborious and slow. Her written sentence consisted of a single word, a verb. Although Anne was someone who once excelled in verbal communication, she could no longer express herself with words. For her, this loss was devastating.

The ability to communicate may come easily to many, but language is a complex process. Words are built of smaller sounds that we must assemble in the correct order—first in our brains and then as we say them aloud. When we speak, one word is usually not enough for communication, so we must rapidly call other words to mind as we articulate our thoughts. Following the rules of grammar, we string words together into sentences, and we add feeling and emphasis by changing our intonation. For most of us, most of the time, words roll off our tongues without much effort, allowing us to express ourselves seamlessly with language.

In the 1860s, physician Pierre Paul Broca described a part of the left frontal lobe that is critical for speech.[119] Now known as Broca's area, this region coordinates the motor systems that direct our lips, tongue, and larynx when we speak. Broca's area is also important for our written output. When people have dysfunction in this region due to FTD, they develop a "non-fluent variant" of primary progressive aphasia. People with this type of aphasia exhibit halting, effortful speech and have difficulty articulating sounds. They also make grammatical errors. While both the semantic variant (the kind that Markus had) and the non-fluent variant of primary progressive aphasia disrupt speech and language, there are significant differences between these syndromes. In contrast to people with the semantic variant who lose knowledge of concepts but speak with ease, like Markus, those with the non-fluent variant retain knowledge of concepts but can no longer communicate with language.

The neuropsychological assessment revealed that Anne had selective difficulties on tests of speech and language. Each word was effortful for Anne to produce, and she struggled with grammar. She used few verbs in her speech and almost always defaulted to nouns. Anne's symptoms and performance on testing were consistent with a non-fluent variant of primary progressive aphasia.

Despite Anne's trouble with speech, other parts of the language system were still unaffected. Her comprehensions of sentences, which engages the posterior parts of the temporal lobes, was good. Anne also did well in other areas of cognitive testing. She had no difficulty determining whether two pictures of faces were similar or different, and she drew even complicated figures with precision. The ability to copy a figure accurately relies on the parietal and occipital lobes at the back of the brain, on the right side more than the left.

As it turned out, Anne's preserved ability to perceive visual information was an important clue about what else was happening in her brain. I would soon learn that there was more to Anne's story than her difficulties with speech.

"Robert, is there anything more I should know about what has been going on with Anne?" I asked.

What Robert revealed next took me by surprise. After Anne retired in her late forties, years before she had any trouble with her speech, she began to paint. Anne's first pieces were simple watercolors of buildings. In one, she painted a monochromatic white house surrounded by a few trees and red roses. She followed this with a picture of her and Robert riding camels during a trip to Egypt. Few of Anne's paintings ever featured people, and even here, she and Robert were not the focus as their faces were hidden by large sunglasses. These realistic, visually pleasing pieces were a prelude to even more groundbreaking work that was yet to come. With the emergence of her new creative abilities, Anne was on her way to becoming a truly extraordinary artist.

Markus and Anne were not the only people to visit our clinic who exhibited newfound artistic abilities in the setting of a neurodegenerative disorder. There was Francisco, a car mechanic from New Mexico. Never interested in art, Francisco unexpectedly took a course in oil painting at a local community center when he was in his late fifties. Around the same time, he began having difficulty finding words and complained, "I can't remember the names of animals or people." Like Markus, Francisco suffered from the semantic variant of primary progressive aphasia. Although Francisco had little formal training in the arts, the quality of his work was astounding. One of his most notable pieces was a surrealistic painting of men from a Navajo tribe dressed

Figure 7.1 Example of a painting drawn in the style of Francisco's paintings. Illustration by Caroline Prioleau.

in traditional garments and set on a rich green background. He also painted churches that he visited in his childhood (Figure 7.1).

Next came Ethan, the director of a successful advertising company and the father of two young children. Around the age of 40, Ethan made a sudden decision to leave his family in California to explore Central America. Ethan was not previously artistic, but during his trip he took hundreds of photographs. While many of his shots focused on lush jungles, others centered on abandoned buildings and stone doors covered by dense rain forest growth. Ethan's trip became a quest to shoot the perfect photograph, and in pursuit of this goal he often captured each scene from multiple angles. Oblivious to the dangers of travel in a civil war zone, Ethan was taken into custody by the military, who suspected that he was working for the local guerrillas. After his release, he returned to his family in California. For a short time, he carved small animals from candle wax. Although Ethan soon lost interest in this activity, he continued to pursue photography until he was diagnosed with the behavioral variant of FTD at age 50.

And then there was Patricia, who started painting in midlife around the same time that she developed behavioral symptoms. The first pieces of art that she made were compelling replicas of works by American-Dutch painters. To embellish each painting, she added her own signature touch. In one reproduction of an idyllic pond scene, she added the image of her beloved family dog to the background. As Patricia's illness progressed, she stopped copying the work of others and developed her own distinctive style. She produced original paintings of houses, horses, and ships. Her final pieces, which were again altogether different from her past work, were slightly distorted portraits of her daughter and granddaughter.

In the years since these individuals first passed through our clinic's doors, we have conducted multiple studies on emergent creativity in dementia. We now know that elevated creativity is relatively common in FTD but is rare in other neurodegenerative disorders such as Alzheimer's disease. The alterations in the brain that must occur for visual creativity to bloom in the setting of dementia are quite specific. Most people with FTD who become visual artists have forms of the disease that affect language or speech.[120] Nearly one-half of the individuals we studied had the semantic variant of primary progressive aphasia, like Markus, and many others had the non-fluent variant like Anne. The remaining few had the behavioral variant of FTD. With only a few exceptions, none of the individuals was a serious artist before there was evidence of aphasia. Their creativity appeared in the setting of the illness. It occurred because of the disease, not despite it!

Neurodegenerative disorders progress slowly, and initial changes in the brain may allow creativity to grow even before clear symptoms have emerged. In the years before they have significant difficulties with language, their visual world becomes more vibrant, and they are capable of incredible feats. Whereas Markus made new associations between ideas because of weakened semantic knowledge, Anne connected her visual and auditory experiences in unique ways. Just as ancient humans linked images and sounds by placing their paintings in parts of the cave with complementary acoustic properties (as described in the Introduction), Anne also linked visual and auditory information in her paintings. By using her paintbrush to translate sounds into shapes and colors, Anne created magnificent art.

"When did Anne produce her most creative artwork?" I asked. Robert told us Anne created her masterpiece, *Unravelling Boléro*, a few years before she developed language symptoms. For two months, she listened to Maurice Ravel's iconoclastic piece, *Boléro*, on repeat as she transformed the composition into a stunning array of images. She used colors and forms to depict the piece's various musical elements as well as her opinions about them.

To represent the meters in *Boléro*, Anne painted a series of adjacent boxes that wound across the canvas in a serpentine fashion. She used dark shapes to signal tonal elements and altered the size of the boxes to indicate changes in volume. The boxes became taller as the notes became louder. While the treble notes hung from the top of the boxes as colorful figures, the bass notes rose from the bottom as complementary monochromatic shapes.

By assigning a specific color to each note, Anne captured the repetitive nature of the music as the same notes and colors reappeared across the painting. The consistency in her color scheme persisted until the 323rd meter, when Ravel made an unexpected key change. Anne marked this transition in her painting by turning to fluorescent pink colors, which continued until the collapse of the music in the final two meters.

Anne followed *Unravelling Boléro* with *Pi (π)*, another painting with a theme of repetition (Figure 7.2). In 1706, mathematician William Jones devised the symbol π to represent the ratio of a circle's circumference to its diameter. The endless and random nature of the numerals in π fascinated Anne. Just as she had used a specific color for each note in *Unravelling Boléro*, she assigned a certain shade to each number in *Pi (π)*. As the same notes appear many times in *Boléro* and the same numbers appear many times in π, the colors that corresponded to the notes and numbers repeated in Anne's paintings and created a dramatic effect. Even before Anne developed symptoms of aphasia, she was drawn to nonverbal information and created novel connections in her paintings between numbers, colors, and sounds.

After *Pi (π)* came other incredible pieces, but the symbolism in Anne's art faded as her brain's speech and language systems declined. As speaking became more difficult, she was increasingly preoccupied with visual information. Anne had always been a keen observer, perhaps due to her background in science, and she began to produce paintings of the natural world that were startlingly precise. First, she created a gouache of rocks, so realistic that it was hard to believe that her painting was not a photograph. Next, she made the *ABC Book of Invertebrates* for her grandchildren in which she associated each letter in the alphabet with a unique invertebrate (Figure 7.3). Anne followed these pieces with a painting of six dying arbutus leaves in various stages of decay, each captured in magnificent detail. In the later stages of her illness, when her aphasia was pronounced, Anne continued to paint, but her focus shifted back to buildings. In one of her last works, she recreated houses that she had seen on a trip to Belgium and the Netherlands, all produced from memory in uncanny detail.

Figure 7.2 Unravelling Boléro by Anne Adams. Image used with permission from Robert Adams.

Figure 7.3 Painting from the *ABC Book of Invertebrates* by Anne Adams. Image used with permission from Robert Adams.

At the time of Anne's visit, we did not understand how a decline in speech allowed her visual creativity to blossom. Over the years, we have found clues to this mystery in our studies of Anne and other artists with FTD. We have also learned more about the association between language and visual abilities from another source entirely. Neurodevelopmental conditions, such as autism and dyslexia, offer an additional window into brain functioning. In children with these conditions, differences in brain development can make cognition, language, or behavior difficult. Despite these challenges, some of these children may also exhibit remarkable talents in other areas. While older adults who lose verbal abilities may acquire visuospatial strengths in later life, children with language challenges in early life may excel in nonverbal abilities such as drawing from a young age.

As I listened to Robert recount Anne's story, my mind wandered back to a young boy whom I met years earlier. Sam was five years old when he and his mother, Heidi, visited me in my office to get my opinion on his diagnosis. Compassionate and optimistic, Heidi exuded a fierce love and devotion for her son. Sam, who had minimal language and limited social skills, had recently been diagnosed with autism.

Sam's primary mode of communication was drawing. Heidi always carried an *Etch A Sketch* with her, and Sam relished the opportunity to draw. Without his *Etch A Sketch*, he was restless and withdrawn. During our three-hour meeting, Sam sketched continuously. His movements were lightning fast as he whipped through one picture after another. The only sounds he made were intermittent squeals of joy. Sam had just seen *Jumanji*, and he drew multiple scenes from the movie on the *Etch A Sketch*, quickly replacing one drawing with another. His memory for visual information was extraordinary.

Heidi brought a large portfolio of Sam's artwork, and together we leafed through his many drawings. By talking with Heidi, I learned that Sam's development was normal until he was 18 months of age, at which point his language and social skills began to recede. With this regression came a compulsive desire to draw, and he created his first pictures when he was around two years old. Drawing soon occupied most of Sam's waking hours, and his earliest drawings were horses. Soon, he created complex, whimsical scenes that included other animals as well as characters from books and movies. I could see from the volume of sketches that Sam had produced that Disney cartoons and Dr. Seuss stories were his favorites. He was prolific, and his drawings were more advanced than any I had seen by a child his age.

Sam had minimal language, but his ability to remember and produce visual information was exceptional. In autism, many children show this type of discrepancy between their verbal and visual abilities. In the 1970s, researcher Lorna Selfe wrote about Nadia, a young girl with autism who had limited language but created beautiful pictures of horses.[121] Child psychiatrist Darold Treffert has also written about people with autism who composed and played music at an expert level.[122] And in his book, *An Anthropologist on Mars,* neurologist Oliver Sacks told the story of Stephen Wiltshire, a young man with autism whose drawings were photograph-like renditions of cities that he had only briefly seen.[123] In our own studies of dyslexia with neurologist Maria Luisa Gorno Tempini, we see a similar pattern. Children with dyslexia, despite having reading challenges, display heightened emotional sensitivity.[124] These strengths in emotional attunement and other nonverbal domains, such as visual and spatial processing, may foster strong interpersonal abilities as well as creativity in dyslexia.

By understanding how language and visual brain systems interact, we can begin to shed light on the origins of nonverbal creativity. Certain brain networks are in competition, and lower activity in one circuit can accentuate functioning in others. Although much remains unknown about brain structure and function in autism and other neurodevelopmental conditions, it is possible that in these children, too, weakness in one brain network allows others to strengthen. In Sam, who had trouble with speech and social interactions, weaker language systems may have given rise to exceptional drawing abilities by allowing the circuits that support visual and spatial processing to flourish.

Sam's drawing obsession and outstanding visual memory led me to wonder whether the posterior areas of his brain, regions that support visual and spatial processing, were hyperactive. Heidi had brought the images from Sam's recent brain scan, and we next reviewed them together. In this type of scan, a rainbow of colors is superimposed on a picture of the brain to show patterns of blood flow. While cooler colors highlight areas with less blood flow and lower activity, warmer colors signal areas with more blood flow and higher activity.

I first looked at the anterior part of the brain. The colors in the frontal lobes were like those seen in children without autism and did not signify anything out of the ordinary. In the posterior regions of the brain, however, the results were striking. Orange and red dominated the parietal and occipital regions in the scan, an unusual pattern to see in a person of any age, let alone in a child.

Sam's scan suggested that there was indeed more blood flow to the back of his brain than to any other regions. Although I could not be certain whether the elevated activity in Sam's visual and spatial systems was the cause or the consequence of his drawing obsession, it was an important clue about his keen ability to remember and recreate what he saw in the world.

Sam's brain scan suggested that his desire to draw was associated with heightened activity in posterior brain regions that support visual and spatial functions. We hypothesized that there may be a similar pattern in Anne's brain. If activity in posterior brain networks climbed as her speech and language systems receded, she may increasingly have been drawn to the visual world. Elevated functioning in visual systems would allow both Anne and Sam to perceive color, texture, and pattern in exacting detail. These accentuated visual experiences might also have inspired them to create in the visual medium. Yet, we still needed additional evidence to elucidate how this might be possible.

Around the time that Anne visited UCSF, there were exciting advances in our understanding of neurodegenerative disorders. Dr. Seeley and neuroscientists Randy Buckner and Michael Greicius had recently found each neurodegenerative disorder attacks select neural circuits but spares others.[125] As the neurons in the affected networks become less connected, they eventually die and cause the brain tissue in that area to shrink. In the early stages of a neurodegenerative disorder, the symptoms that a person experiences show a similar specificity and reflect the circuits that are deteriorating. Often, these symptoms reflect loss of function in brain systems that help us to move, think, and feel. In the field of neurology, the idea that neurodegenerative disorders disrupt specific brain networks was novel at the time. The existing dogma had always been that dementia affects the whole brain and causes widespread loss of abilities. But, at least in the initial stages of neurodegenerative disorders, this is not the case.

Remarkably, loss of function is not the only change that can occur in neurodegenerative disorders. Dr. Seeley and neuroscientist Helen Zhou later discovered that, as certain networks became less connected, others became *more* connected.[126] In Alzheimer's disease, brain networks that support episodic memory decline, and people have trouble remembering recent events. As the integrity of these systems fades, however, the connectivity of brain networks that support emotional empathy becomes stronger. Consistent with these findings, we have found individuals with early Alzheimer's disease have higher emotional empathy than healthy older adults without the disease, and this emotional sensitivity grows as the disease progresses.[127] These gains in emotional sensitivity may even begin before other cognitive symptoms have made themselves clear.[128]

Anne's decline in speech was an isolated problem when her symptoms started. And amazingly, her burgeoning artistic talents preceded her changes in speech. In some ways, Anne and Sam had similar difficulties with communication albeit their troubles emerged at different ends of the lifespan. They also shared similar strengths and an intense interest in the visual world. If the activity pattern in Sam's brain scan was illustrative of the changes in Anne's brain, then it would be likely that she would also have elevated activity in posterior brain regions that support visual and spatial abilities. Although we did not yet know whether this was the case, a brain scan would shed light on this question.

After hearing Robert's story, Dr. Seeley and I reviewed Anne's recent brain MRI. Consistent with her symptoms, the areas in her scan with the most dramatic tissue loss were regions that produce speech. The area with the most notable atrophy was the left frontal lobe, in a part that included Broca's area.

Years before Anne developed language symptoms, she sought medical attention for hearing problems and headaches and underwent a series of brain MRIs at that time. Luckily for us, and for science, Robert saved these scans and gave us copies. When we compared Anne's earlier MRIs to her most recent one, we saw something incredible. Even five years before Anne had any trouble with her speech, she had mild tissue loss in the left frontal lobe. Despite having changes in brain regions that support speech production, Anne used her strong intellect and robust cognitive reserve to compensate for any difficulties.

During the years when Anne's language networks were faltering but her speech was still intact, she became an artist. Was it possible that early changes in the language areas of her brain had unlocked activity in the posterior regions that support visual and spatial processing? One of the early MRIs that Anne completed confirmed our hunch. In this scan, there was greater blood flow in the right parietal regions than in other areas--the same pattern I had seen in Sam's scan. Although the similarity between their scans was intriguing, we still needed to conduct quantitative studies to see whether other people with FTD who became artists also showed a similar pattern. Such studies soon followed.

After meeting Anne, Dr. Seeley conducted quantitative studies of her brain. To measure the changes in her brain's posterior areas, he compared her early scans to those of healthy people her age who did not have a neurodegenerative disorder.[129] These analyses revealed that Anne had larger volume in the right posterior parts of the brain than the healthy individuals. Could these regions have grown in the setting of Anne's neurodegenerative disorder? We suspected it was possible.

In more recent research, Dr. Seeley and neurologist Adit Friedberg expanded on this work by studying more people with FTD who, like Anne, exhibited gains in visual creativity and became artists.[130] They saw a pattern in the brain scans of these individuals that resembled what we had seen in Anne. As expected, the people with FTD had atrophy in the frontal and anterior temporal lobes. What was more surprising was that those who had more severe atrophy in these anterior areas of the brain had greater activity in the posterior regions. Drs. Seeley and Friedberg also found another striking result. The people with FTD who became artists had higher connectivity between the occipital lobe and a specific part of the motor system—the part that controls the right hand—than those who did not become artists. This strong connection may have allowed these individuals, motivated by their increasingly powerful visual experiences, to create art with their right hand. As they practiced and honed their craft, the connectivity between these areas may have gotten even stronger, further driving their ability to produce visual art with exceptional skill.

Creativity requires motivation and perseverance. Becoming a talented artist is not a passive process and often begins with a drive, even an obsession, that leads to repetition of a specific activity. Sometimes, this drive for repetition is evident in the artwork itself. When researching Anne's painting, *Unravelling Boléro*, we discovered something else that was truly unexpected. About three years after Ravel composed *Boléro*, he also developed a progressive aphasia, just like Anne. Though a century separated their lives, these artists had similar speech and language symptoms due to progressive dysfunction in the same left frontal regions of the brain. Both Anne and Ravel experienced a burst of creativity in the initial stages of the disease before they began to struggle with speech. During this early period, they both produced original creations that diverged from their previous works. *Boléro*, which was unlike anything that he had made before or would ever produce again, puzzled Ravel himself. For Ravel, *Boléro* represented a distinctive style of composing that he described as an "experiment in sound" and "orchestral tissue without music." The repetition in the piece was unmistakable and drew Anne into the depths of its musical structure as she created her own *Unravelling Boléro*. For reasons that we still do not understand, the changes that occurred in the brains of both Anne and Ravel inspired them to create works of art that reverberated with repetition.

Many of the artists with FTD who came to our clinic became visual artists. In these individuals, degeneration of the left frontal and anterior temporal lobes disrupted language and speech but accentuated activity in the right posterior parts of the brain that are critical for creating visual art. Although most began to paint, others started sculpting or quilting. Their pieces, like those by Markus, often featured bright colors including purple and yellow. Other people with similar brain changes developed a heightened interest in other nonverbal pursuits such as music or sports. There was the businessman who became known in midlife for his composition of quartets. Despite his early musical training, he had never composed previously. There was also the teacher who had little prior interest in music or sports but then mastered playing the piano and ping pong.

In the people with FTD who had degeneration in the right frontal and anterior temporal lobes, verbal creativity was more likely to occur as posterior circuits in the left hemisphere that support language became hyperactive. There was the telephone line worker who crafted limericks. Her experimentation with prose and rhyme represented an unexpected form of verbal creativity that she had never exhibited. There was the flight attendant who began to write poetry, the minister who created sermons littered with puns, and the cab driver who told tales full of word play. The quality of these pieces varied, ranging from mundane to brilliant, which likely reflected something about their baseline brain wiring. Just as the richness of the soil in a garden influences the heartiness of the plants that grow there, the complexity of each artist's unique brain circuitry prior to their illness likely shaped the work they created in the setting of FTD.

The first symptoms of a neurodegenerative disorder usually reflect the loss of function in specialized brain networks, but in some people, gains in creativity may precede the emergence of cognitive symptoms. Of course, it would be preferable for people to exhibit elevated creativity without going on to experience dementia. With the development of new medicines, the day is coming when we will be able to halt the disease when creativity has climbed, but cognitive deficits have not yet surfaced. While we will never ignore a person's lost abilities—those, unfortunately, are the hallmark features of neurodegenerative disorders—it is critical that we recognize their strengths. As Anne taught us, appreciating the skills and talents of people with neurodegenerative disorders can help to preserve their sense of purpose and well-being.

If we dig deep and ask the right questions, each person with FTD teaches us important lessons about the social brain. The stories of people with FTD have offered important insights into the brain systems underlying creativity—a core human ability that is present in all of us but can be hard for some of us to access. With practice, we can unlock our creative potential and allow ourselves to see the world with fresh eyes. Novel ways of thinking spur innovations and are critical for breakthroughs in art, science, technology, and many other fields. Creativity, which first began to flourish in our early societies, continues to lie at the heart of who we are and why we succeed.

8 Cultivating the Social Brain

Since our ancestors first settled in stable societies, the social brain has played an instrumental role in human life. The social brain allowed ancient humans to live and work together in harmony, which led to advances in language and the arts. There are many differences between the social worlds of ancient and modern humans, but people in early communities grappled with many of the same matters that we do today. They, too, struggled to create equitable societies, to care for others while looking out for their own needs, and to communicate their feelings and ideas. The social brain has been essential for addressing these issues and continues to be the source of our most remarkable achievements.

But the social brain also has a dark side. While the social brain can generate virtuous feelings of compassion, affection, and gratitude, it can also create negative feelings. Hatred, contempt, and jealousy are emotions that legal scholar john a. powell believes are at the root of "othering," a divisive practice in which people are considered less than others because of their perceived negative qualities.[131] Othering creates painful feelings of subordination, inequity, and shame. In its most extreme forms, othering can lead to dehumanization as well as cruelty.

Whereas humans thousands of years ago only knew their families and people in their local communities, we humans in the modern age have more complex social networks. Our social connections now span the physical and virtual worlds, and new relationships are at our fingertips with the help of technology. With a few keystrokes on our computers or phones, we can interact with people around the globe. We can learn about their lives and opinions and share their experiences without even leaving our homes. Although having these social connections has its benefits, it can also have undesirable consequences. The algorithms that populate our news and social media feeds with content create echo chambers that validate, but do not challenge, our opinions. When people from different ideologies and cultures cannot understand another group's viewpoints or find common ground, othering and polarization increase. Extreme views on either side of a debate undermine trust between individuals and hinder progress on critical societal issues.

DOI: 10.4324/9781003502357-10

We can counteract these negative influences by taking some simple steps. As we described in this book, our social brain circuits expand and bring goodness into the world when we care for others. Curt, Susan, Ellen, Deepak, James, and Robert were devoted caregivers whose social brains developed as they continued to nurture their loved ones. Imagine the possibilities if we each did a little more to cultivate the networks in our social brains. But can we create a world where fairness, empathy, respect, self-awareness, openness, and creativity are the norm? This is a major dilemma that will require careful thought to solve, and people around the globe will need to participate if we are to make progress. Humans are capable of impressive growth, and here we consider some ways that we can all build our social brain circuitry.

Building Social Relationships

The need to belong is a fundamental human motivation.[132] We form close connections with a small inner circle, but we also maintain a wider network of more casual affiliations. As described by sociologist Mark Granovetter, strong relationships are critical for meeting our emotional needs, but weak social ties—counterintuitive as it may seem—are also important and help us to feel part of a larger interconnected world.[133] A friendly glance from a stranger, as well as a heartfelt conversation with a confidante, can increase feelings of belonging and well-being. As a key source of ideas and resources, relationships also serve practical purposes and allow us to transfer information and to influence people both near and far.

Although physical safety and other basic needs, such as food and shelter, are of paramount importance, we also want to feel that we belong in our communities. People experience a sense of belonging when they feel like they are an important part of the systems and environments in which they live and work. Feeling that we belong with different people—such as our families, friends, local communities, and cultural groups—and in different places—such as at school or our place of employment—yields numerous benefits.[134] It feels good to belong, and the positive emotions that we experience when we are part of a group solidify our connections to those people and places. Belonging is associated with advantages across the lifespan including better motivation and academic outcomes in children[135] and better well-being and physical health in older adults.[136]

Despite our powerful desire to belong, many people lack social relationships. Some individuals do not have the relationships they once had because their social brains have changed. Jaime and Thomas experienced increasing social isolation because FTD led them to stop interacting with others in kind ways. As a result of their inconsiderate behavior, many family members and friends became more distant or severed ties with them completely. Social isolation has negative effects on brain functioning and likely exacerbated the pace of their disease.

Other people lack social relationships for different reasons, and feelings of loneliness often become much more common as we age. Studies from around the globe find that social isolation, loneliness, and living alone can worsen health and increase risk of mortality, especially in older adults.[137] Although short-lived feelings of loneliness can motivate us to seek out others, those who feel lonely over sustained periods of time have higher rates of depression, poorer quality of sleep, worse executive function, lower cardiovascular function, diminished immunity, higher stress hormones, and more rapid cognitive decline.[138] Loneliness makes people attentive to potential threats in the environment and prone to negative experiences such as social rejection, paranoia, and suffering.[139] Finding ways to integrate even the most marginalized members of our communities will be important if we hope to reduce loneliness and to achieve truly inclusive societies.

We can enhance feelings of belonging by building social relationships. It is not only the quantity of our relationships that matters, however, but also the quality. We form strong social bonds through frequent and varied interactions with others, and relationships deepen when we feel validated and understood after disclosing our innermost thoughts and feelings.[140] Over time, people in close relationships become interdependent and mutually influence each other's thoughts, feelings, and actions.[141] Strong social bonds are key sources of emotional support and positive emotions that buffer us from persistent negative emotions and stress.

Fostering Well-Being

Supportive relationships not only help us to belong but are also crucial for well-being. Well-being is a broad term that refers to the positive feelings of engagement, purpose, and meaning that we experience in life.[142] People with greater well-being are engaged in various communities and activities and report high satisfaction with their life circumstances. When people feel good about these areas of their lives, they also usually endorse strong feelings of happiness and other positive emotions. Positive emotions feel good and serve many crucial functions in everyday life. As an antidote to negative emotions, positive emotions slow our heart and breathing and help us to recover from moments of anger, fear, and sadness.[143] We are more likely to experience positive emotions when self-protection is not our focus. These pleasant feelings motivate us to engage with others, to plan for the future, and to take steps to achieve our goals.[144] They are critical for us to survive and thrive.

People who experience positive emotions with ease are often optimistic, likable, confident, sociable, and flexible. Each caregiver in this book exhibited these traits. Although at times they struggled, their positive attitude helped them to adapt to the changing needs of their loved ones and to overcome daunting circumstances. Positive emotions can help us to find success when life is difficult, but the association between positive emotions and success is a two-way street. While individuals high in well-being and happiness tend to have certain advantages (such as more stable marriages, higher incomes, and greater creativity) compared to their less happy counterparts, having success in these areas also brings them more happiness.[145] In other words, successful people are more often happy, but happy people are also more likely to find success. Although success in life is often associated with achievements and money, in societies where people have their basic needs met, income does not have a strong association with well-being.[146] What really brings people joy is their social relationships.

We can all cultivate well-being by strengthening our social relationships and enhancing our positive emotions. One way we can work toward both goals is by helping other people. Being generous elicits positive feelings because giving to others activates reward systems in the brain.[147] Performing random acts of kindness—such as spending money on someone, making charitable donations, and supporting others in need—also increases well-being and happiness.[148] As with any good habit, finding activities that evoke positive emotions becomes easier with practice and time.

Creating a Meaningful Life

A happy life, though enticing, is different from a meaningful life. When our needs and desires are satisfied, we are likely to feel happy, but our lives may still lack the meaning and purpose that we seek. A sense of purpose helps us to identify goals that are personally significant and motivates us to achieve those goals in ways that are authentic.[149] People with a clear sense of purpose can move from one goal to the next, or even juggle multiple goals at once. They also can generate successful plans and inspire others to help them achieve success. Those without a clear sense of direction, in contrast, may drift listlessly because it is difficult for them to know what to do next after achieving their goals.[150] A sense of purpose is not just an important motivator when we are young but also helps us to maintain health and well-being as we age. Older adults who continue to live meaningful lives have better daily functioning, cognitive performance, and mood.[151]

Unlike happiness, which is focused on the present, meaningfulness requires a more holistic and longitudinal outlook on life.[152] Activities that foster meaningfulness are those that we pursue with the future in mind, but they are not always enjoyable in the present. Individuals who feel they have more meaningful lives report feeling more anxiety, stress, and worry than those who describe their lives as less meaningful.[153] For most people, close relationships are essential for a meaningful life.[154] As meaningfulness is more related to what we give to others rather than to what we take from them, many people find meaning when they dedicate themselves to other people. Working to create a good life for one's family and helping strangers are common activities that foster a sense of purpose and also benefit one's mental and physical health.[155]

When caring for family members, people not only find meaning in caring for their children but also in caring for their aging parents. For caregivers of people with neurodegenerative disorders, witnessing the decline of a loved one can be devastating yet can also provide opportunities for personal growth. Curt's relentless devotion to Jaime highlighted the powerful human desire to protect others, but he made enormous sacrifices to stay by her side. In the long run, the responsibility that Curt felt for Jaime allowed him to become even more patient, ingenious, and nurturing. The sense of accomplishment that he felt from caring for her provided him with renewed dedication and energy. For Curt, helping Jaime was not just good for her but was also good for him. His sense of purpose helped him to handle stressful situations and to persevere.[156] Although caregivers, like Curt, often develop numerous admirable skills, many receive no financial support for their efforts. Our societies must value and compensate unpaid caregivers, who collectively volunteer billions of hours each year, for the essential services they provide to our most vulnerable community members.

Finding Compassion and Awe

Compassion is a form of empathy that inspires us to relieve others' suffering.[157] As we feel empathy more easily when we see how we are similar to others, we can foster compassion by finding areas of shared interest and experience. Even if we strive to see the world from others' perspectives and to care about their struggles, however, empathy burnout is rampant across the globe. In the modern age, stories and images of suffering bombard us on television and the internet. Despite having more exposure to others' lives, we often feel numb, disconnected, and powerless to help. Feelings of hopelessness put us at risk of losing compassion, but there are steps we can take to continue to care for others. Savoring positive moments and doing kind things for others are examples of small acts that boost compassion and help us to feel more socially connected.[158] Over time, these practices can yield meaningful improvements in mood and life satisfaction as well as gains in empathy.

Another way to foster compassion is to increase our experiences of awe. Awe is a positive emotion that we feel when we are in the presence of vast things that we do not immediately understand.[159] We feel awe in response to physical vastness—such as when we look up into a starry night sky or take in the panoramic view from a mountaintop. We can also feel awe in response to the tiny details of the world around us such as the intricate patterns of the veins on a leaf, the majestic coloring of an orchid, or the synchronized movements of birds in flight. Nature is an easy place to experience awe, but art, religion, science, sporting events, concerts, and political events are also common places that people feel this emotion. When we feel awe, we must adjust our mental schemas to take in new information that we did not know or think was possible.[160] During experiences of awe, our attention also shifts away from the self and promotes compassion by motivating us to attend to the needs of others. Feelings of awe promote a "small self," which means we feel smaller yet more connected to the larger universe around us. Without a narrow focus on ourselves, we can see things in perspective and become more aware of the roles we play in our communities.

Some people experience awe more easily than others, but there are things we all can do to make our chances of feeling awe more likely. In one of our studies, we investigated whether we could increase experiences of awe in healthy older adults through "awe walks."[161] We randomly assigned participants to one of two experimental groups. Participants in both groups took weekly 15-minute outdoor walks for eight weeks. They could walk wherever they chose—in a park, city, forest, farm, suburb, or anywhere else (Figure 8.1). There was a crucial difference between the instructions that we gave each group, however. Only participants in the "awe walk" group learned a few ways to foster experiences of awe. We asked them to tap into their childlike sense of wonder during their walks and to approach the world with fresh eyes. Participants in the awe walk group were encouraged to go somewhere new each time if they could, but this was not a requirement.

Throughout the study, the participants rated how strongly they experienced a variety of positive and negative emotions each day. When we later analyzed these data, the results were striking. To confirm that awe walks were an effective way to elevate awe, we checked to make sure that the participants in the awe walk group reported higher feelings of awe during their walks than the participants in the control walk group. This was indeed the case. We also discovered that the participants who took awe walks reported greater increases in prosocial positive emotions (including compassion, admiration, and gratitude) and feelings of social connection than those who took control walks. Many of the beneficial feelings that the awe walks evoked even persisted on days when the participants did not take a walk.

Figure 8.1 Participants in both groups took walks in a variety of locations.

We asked participants to do one more thing during each walk—to take a selfie. We used these photographs for two purposes. First, we examined whether those in the awe walk group displayed bigger smiles over the course of the study than those who took control walks. We coded the intensity of the smiles in each of the photographs and found that this was the case. Next, we used the selfies to test whether awe walks promoted a small self. To do this, we traced the silhouette of the participant in each photograph and computed a ratio of the number of pixels that participant filled with themselves versus the background scenery. Over time, participants in the awe walks group filled less of their photographs with themselves and more of the photographs with the background—evidence that suggested awe walks did foster a small self! (Figure 8.2).

Figure 8.2 Participants in the awe walk group had a smaller self in their selfies at the end of the study (Week 8) than at the beginning of the study (Week 1). Participants in the control walk group did not show a difference in this measure over the course of the study.

Compassion and awe are essential emotions in the modern age. As technology increasingly dominates our daily lives, it is easy to overlook the importance of feeling connected to the social and natural worlds. Cultivating compassion is important for all of us but may be especially important for people with high levels of negative emotions and stress such as caregivers and people with dementia. For these individuals, practices that promote compassion may be especially powerful by helping them to feel less isolated and by promoting other positive emotions such as gratitude.

Feeling Gratitude

Gratitude is a positive emotion that we experience when we are the recipient of benevolence. Highly prized across spiritual and religious traditions, gratitude reminds us how fortunate we are and encourages us to appreciate the simple things in life.[162] Receiving a gift may easily spark gratitude, but we also feel grateful for other positive things in life such as good health in ourselves and in our families. When we appreciate and savor life's small pleasures, we may seek more opportunities to give back to others some of the goodness that we have received from the world.[163]

In our everyday lives, social relationships are a common source of gratitude. When others are kind and responsive to our needs, our gratitude grows as does our motivation to be generous and cooperative. Feelings of gratitude make us more willing to offer emotional support and to go out of our way for others in need.[164] Expressions of gratitude can strengthen relationships, rekindle affection, and motivate reciprocal actions in people who have grown distant.[165] We admire and feel more connected to people who communicate their gratitude to us,[166] and witnessing others expressing gratitude can have a ripple effect and cause gratitude to spread across social networks.[167] With just a little effort, gratitude and its myriad positive effects can easily multiply across people and places.

We can foster gratitude by taking some simple actions. Practices such as counting blessings and journaling about the things for which we are grateful are effective ways to increase gratitude in everyday life.[168] When gratitude grows, optimism and positivity also bloom. In terms of its physical health benefits, gratitude is associated with lower blood pressure, depression, and anxiety as well as better sleep quality and immune functioning.[163] Gratitude not only promotes positive interactions when times are good but also shapes our responses to unpleasant life events. It seems that individuals higher in gratitude are equipped to see even challenging situations in a positive light. They are skilled at reframing negative events and seeing them as an opportunity for learning.[169] This ability to see even hardships as a chance for personal growth and improvement is a principal element of resilience, the topic we turn to next.

Bolstering Resilience

Positive emotions like gratitude help us to reduce and recover from negative emotions, but we cannot prevent bad things from happening. Unpleasant experiences are unavoidable in life, but many people show remarkable resilience even in the face of traumatic events. After a period of acute distress, people with high resilience bounce back and maintain good health trajectories.[170] They not only lack mental and physical symptoms after the negative event, but they also continue to have positive emotional experiences.

By becoming more resilient, we can prepare ourselves for whatever challenges life throws our way. Even in people with a neurodegenerative disorder, some are more resilient than others to the changes that occur in the brain. Education, a healthy diet, good quality sleep, physical activity, and cognitive stimulation make our brains more robust and protect us from decline. Although these biological and cognitive factors are important, much of our resilience depends on our social relationships. In adults (as well as children), supportive parental and peer relationships are key for fostering resilience to adversity or tragedy.[171] We turn to others when we need someone to comfort us, and feelings of emotional closeness help us to weather tough times by letting us know that we have someone in our corner. Some individuals even end up in a better place after trauma by making a conscious effort to integrate what they have learned from their experience as they move forward.[172] This ability—to find the positive aspects of even unpleasant moments—is a key element of wisdom, a topic that we return to later in this chapter.

People who are resilient have many tools at their disposal to manage strong emotions. As we learned in Chapter 3, we can use different tactics to shape which emotions we have and when we have them via a process known as emotion regulation.[58] We can distract ourselves from things that elicit the negative feelings that we would rather avoid, or we can engage in activities where the positive feelings that we desire are likely to arise. By focusing our attention on pleasant details in the environment or changing how we think about a situation, we can work to create the emotional lives that we seek. As there is no one-size-fits-all emotion regulation strategy, each of these approaches might be more effective in some settings than others. To behave in ways that align with our beliefs and values, we must be able to shift our mindset and integrate feedback to be effective in each situation.[173]

For many, resilience is rooted in the belief that overcoming obstacles and securing resources today will help them to have a better tomorrow.[174] This hope inspires them to persevere through the hard periods of life. As time passes, we make meaning of our experiences by creating stories that link the past, present, and future.[175] The stories that we tell ourselves about our lives not only help us to accept the fact that suffering is an inevitable part of the human experience but also help us to know ourselves, another key human ability.

Knowing Yourself

For millennia, humans have strived to know ourselves and to act in ways that are consistent with our "true self." Even the ancient Greeks stressed the importance of "knowing thyself," inscribing this dictum in the temple of Apollo. In 350 BCE, Aristotle wrote about "eudaimonia" and emphasized that behaving in ways that reflect one's true nature is the foundation of excellence and fulfillment in life.[176] Modern philosophers and psychologists continue to stress the importance of authentic self-expression in human flourishing, with self-awareness and authenticity essential elements of eudaimonia.[177]

To be authentic, we must have a sense of who we are, but truly knowing oneself is challenging. As we described in Chapter 5, the self has many layers. Some layers of the self are public facing, but others remain private, secured in the inner sanctuaries of the mind. Although suffering may ensue if we create lives that do not align with our true self, figuring out who we are is a mysterious process that remains opaque for many. Being authentic has many benefits if we can achieve it. People who feel they are authentic have greater clarity in their self-concept and higher self-esteem and well-being.[178] Authenticity is a social process, however, and is ultimately judged by others. We may think that we are authentic, but if those around us disagree, then we are not.

One way that we know ourselves is through our emotions. Tracking our feelings is something that only we can do, and putting our feelings into words is an effective way to understand our emotions. People vary in how well they can verbalize their experiences.[179] While some use precise language to label how they feel, others use coarse descriptions that lack specificity. Whereas one person might discriminate among feelings of "joy," "glee," "elation," "jubilation," and "delight," another might just always report feeling "good." Having more refined emotional experiences and more nuanced words to express one's feelings is associated with numerous health benefits.[180] People who make more fine-grained distinctions among their experiences are better able to manage strong emotions and have larger volume in brain regions that support emotion regulation.[181] Taken together, these studies suggest that using words to label feelings helps us to gain control over internal states that can sometimes overwhelm us.

Language not only enables us to name our feelings but also helps us to remember events in an organized way. Like any good story, each tale that we tell ourselves has the goal of organizing the key events in a logical order.[182] When we express our experiences with words—either orally or in writing— we are more likely to understand our thoughts and feelings and to find resolutions to our problems.[183] By articulating our emotions, we are better able to feel a greater sense of control over our lives and to know ourselves.

Promoting Openness and Creativity

To know who we are, we must know what is real, but to be creative, we must suspend reality and imagine new possibilities. When people think of creativity, they often think of those rare individuals who are truly extraordinary in their field, often in art or science. These individuals are born with unique gifts, but exceptional talent reflects the contributions of both genes and experiences. For most, there is a long incubation period (often ten years!) that is characterized by immersion and intense practice. During this critical time, they develop the skills or knowledge that they need to produce true innovations.[184] Most of us exhibit creativity on a smaller scale in everyday life. This type of creativity shares many elements of the creativity that lies at the heart of outstanding achievements. The origins of both types of creativity, though seemingly ethereal, are not as mysterious as they appear. Creativity is built from simple cognitive processes including divergent thinking and problem-solving and, as such, is attainable for all of us.[185]

People who are creative exhibit openness to new experiences and tend to be more positive and passionate about their work and lives.[186] Positive emotions fuel curiosity and exploration by broadening our minds and inspiring new ideas and questions.[187] We can think of more creative connections between topics when we experience even brief positive states, but certain positive emotions, such as awe, may foster creativity more than others. As described above, during awe we adjust our views of the world, a process that naturally encourages flexible thinking. Although it is possible that awe walks might offer an extra boost for creativity, even walking on its own—and especially walking outside—can get the creative juices flowing.[188] During walks and other forms of exercise, we can think about the future and ponder recent experiences. Sometimes, this process of introspection can lead us to have insights into our problems or to forge new connections between ideas.

The benefits of creativity do not stop there. Unlike many cognitive abilities, creativity remains largely stable as we age and may even peak in the later decades of life for some of us.[189] As we saw in Chapters 6 and 7, as Markus and Anne became open to new possibilities, they became even more creative and produced exceptional artistic pieces. If each of us continues to pursue activities that benefit our mood and motivate divergent thinking, we will likely enjoy our creative pursuits into our very last years.

Educating the Whole Brain

Debate has long surrounded the nature of intelligence, and our societies and schools still overlook the importance of creativity and other functions of the social brain. While many now agree that there are multiple forms of intelligence, schools continue to emphasize training in language and math skills that rely predominantly on the brain's left hemisphere.[190] By the time children reach kindergarten, the "three R's"—reading, writing, and arithmetic—

are already the primary focus of the academic curriculum, and there is an increasing emphasis on test-taking skills rather than creative thinking. Training in language, mathematics, and science is essential for young learners to hone their analytical thinking. Proficiency in these areas builds brain circuits that we use throughout our lives and that protect us from cognitive decline as we age. The formal education that we receive in school is critical for brain development. Neurologist Elisa de Paula França Resende has shown that people with even just one year of schooling have higher brain connectivity than those who never went to school and cannot read.[191] As reading opens new avenues for learning and information gathering, literacy is critical for building robust neural circuits throughout the brain. Reading (especially fiction) also sparks imagination and builds empathy for others.[192]

Many schools praise students with strong left-hemisphere abilities. Children who are exceptional in reading, spelling, writing, and math may be deemed "gifted" at an early age and placed in special classes or schools. When children have notable trouble in any of these areas, they may be evaluated and diagnosed with a specific learning disorder such as dyslexia. Why then is no learning disorder diagnosed when children have significant difficulty with drawing, sculpting, or rhythm? Many of these nonverbal abilities, like our social and emotional abilities, depend on the right hemisphere. Excellence in these areas is often overlooked as a sign of intelligence. When school budgets are tight, art, music, and socioemotional learning are usually the first courses to be cut because these subjects are considered less critical for success.

Social, emotional, and creative skills are often underappreciated in our education systems but are essential for humans to thrive. While there is growing interest in socioemotional learning in elementary, middle, and high schools, there are still enormous opportunities for growth in this area. New courses and activities that weave together fact-based learning with human values and creativity have the potential to develop circuits in both hemispheres of the brain while also increasing feelings of belonging and social connectedness. The possibilities for human achievement would be endless if we could leverage each person's talents and foster development of the whole brain.

Celebrating Our Strengths

We all have our own unique brain wiring that shapes what we can accomplish. Understanding where our individual strengths lie is as important as acknowledging—even appreciating—our weaknesses. Each of us has enormous potential, but not everyone can be a poet, baseball pitcher, sculptor, social worker, astrophysicist, ballet dancer, or surgeon. In some people, circuits that support language or mathematics are highly developed. And in others, circuits that promote music, visual arts, or engineering are the most complex. Still others have strong circuits in the social brain, which makes them intensely interested in other people. We flourish when we can harness our strengths, whatever they may be, while acknowledging the areas where we still have room for growth. Sam's mother, Heidi, was exemplary in celebrating her son's artistic talent while also seeking help for his difficulties in social behavior and language. We are born with strengths in certain areas, but our life experiences also influence our brain development. The plasticity of our brains is greatest when we are young, and as children we tend to pursue activities that we are good at and that we enjoy. Practice, combined with curiosity and discipline, enables us to achieve and maintain excellence. As we hone our skills, we may strengthen certain circuits but turn down competing circuits. Our experiences constantly reshape our brains, so it may be necessary to inhibit certain circuits to allow others to flourish. As we get older, we focus less on attaining our goals and become better at savoring the journey. Engaging in activities that we find fulfilling is important riding out the inevitable storms in life and for aging well.[193]

Seeing the good in ourselves, and in others, may be essential for our own well-being and for the longevity of the social brain. When we appreciate that our family members and friends have strengths and weaknesses that reflect differences in their brain wiring, we can be more understanding when challenges arise. Societies that value all citizens for their unique gifts will be better prepared to solve the world's most difficult problems.

Recent decades have brought numerous amazing discoveries about the social brain. We are in an exciting era of neuroscience research that will continue to progress at a rapid pace. With technical advances in neuroimaging, genetics, and artificial intelligences, it is increasingly possible to track our every thought, feeling, and movement. Although these technologies have great potential to do good, they also have the capacity to do harm. Before incorporating these tools into our lives, each of us will need to scrutinize their costs and benefits.

A better understanding of the social brain pushes science forward but can also enrich each of our lives. Learning about the social brain should start in families and continue in schools, workplaces, and places of worship. Finding new ways to use awe to spark curiosity in the classroom or to cultivate gratitude for our neighbors to encourage friendships will help us all to grow as social beings. We can use knowledge of the social brain to become more empathic parents, friends, neighbors, and colleagues. Biology, in addition to life experiences, influences our thoughts and feelings. By incorporating information about how the social brain operates into our everyday interactions, we might gain insights into others' behavior.

The neuroscience of social behavior also needs to play a more central role in our societies. It is not only schools but also health care settings that pay little attention to the importance of our social brain circuits in our physical and mental health. The arts, likewise, seldom reference the relation of the brain to social behavior. If novels, movies, television shows, plays, and musicals embraced and integrated the expanding neuroscience of social brain, there would be many more opportunities for us all to learn. Not only could broader audiences have access to the latest neuroscientific research presented in an entertaining format, but artists could help to broaden the topics that neuroscientists prioritize in their studies by offering new perspectives. A new dialogue about neuroscience could permeate our everyday lives and help everyone to deepen their understanding of themselves and each other. Tighter connections between the scientific and artistic communities never cease to produce original creations from which we all benefit.

As computer-based systems replace face-to-face interactions, humans need to find new ways to develop meaningful social connections. Our brains are wired to connect with others, and our need to form meaningful relationships will not change. Having stronger social brains will benefit us as individuals who care about our own needs and as citizens who care about the needs of others. To fortify our social brain circuits, we must deepen our relationships and imagine new possibilities. The mysteries of the social brain have the power to unlock the solutions that will help us to create a better world for people today and for those yet to come.

Epilogue

The frontal and anterior temporal lobes are key areas in the social brain. These structures, and their connected circuits, make us who we are and underlie our incredible capacities for emotions, communication, and creativity. Many of the stories that we shared in this book focused on FTD, a neurodegenerative disorder that targets systems in the social brain. Like other neurological and psychiatric conditions, FTD has taught us many important lessons about how the social brain operates. Although we have learned much about the biology of our most human abilities, much of the social brain remains shrouded in mystery.

In the social brain, circuits in the right hemisphere are especially important for our relationships. Expansion of brain networks in the right frontal and anterior temporal lobes allowed ancient humans to develop new social abilities. They used their sophisticated social skills to form close friendships and to build stable communities. Living in groups not only helped them to acquire physical resources but also provided them with a wellspring of emotional support. People in these early societies needed a strong capacity for empathy to ensure they were sensitive to the needs of others and self-awareness to remain cognizant of their own feelings and actions. An appreciation for fairness and a healthy respect for social rules were essential for maintaining social harmony.

When FTD attacks circuits in the right side of the social brain, social behavior changes. Regardless of whether people had weak or strong interpersonal skills prior to their illness, their ability to care for others withers when the disease takes hold. Jaime may have been insensitive to others from adolescence, but Thomas, Clark, and Amit were charming until midlife when FTD began. For each of these individuals, the loss of function in social brain circuits in the right hemisphere had devastating effects on their relationships and, ultimately, on their survival.

FTD can also disrupt the circuits in the social brain that support language and creativity. When FTD disrupts the left frontal and anterior temporal lobes, people lose their ability to communicate with words. Some people with FTD who lose speech and language become more sensitive to what they see and gain visual creativity. Anne and Markus had decline in different circuits in the left side of the brain that support communication. Whereas Anne struggled to produce speech because of atrophy in the left frontal lobe, Markus lost semantic knowledge and no longer knew the meanings of words and objects because of atrophy in the left anterior temporal lobe.

As their speech and language degraded, Anne and Markus both became increasingly preoccupied with the nonverbal, visual world and began to paint. Preservation of the posterior regions in the right hemisphere allowed them each to think in colors, shapes, and patterns rather than in words, sentences, and grammar. Although Markus did not attempt to communicate deeper messages to his audience in his paintings, in her early works, Anne used her paint strokes to articulate her opinions about sounds and numbers. When her symptoms became more severe, however, she no longer used images to express what she could not with speech. Instead, she recreated objects that she observed in the natural world, just as the ancient humans first did.

Anne, Markus, and the others with FTD all developed prominent symptoms in specific areas of speech, language, or behavior. To illustrate the neuroanatomical underpinnings of the key changes in this book, we focused on one primary symptom and a limited number of brain regions in each chapter. In reality, most of the individuals we described exhibited many of the changes in social behavior that we discussed throughout the book. As FTD progresses, the disease eventually affects most, if not all, regions in the social brain. Thus, it is unlikely that any one person has isolated problems in fairness, empathy, respect, or self-awareness, and more likely that they have alterations in all these abilities.

Even today, we are often taught that our experiences and life circumstances determine our behavior. Yes, that is true, but there is more. Biology is also crucial. The fact that the brain is the source of social behavior is still a relatively novel concept in neuroscience. Dr. Benson, who taught me invaluable lessons about the importance of the frontal and anterior temporal lobes in social behavior, was ahead of his time. He reasoned that changes in social behavior, like changes in movement or thinking, also reflect alterations in specific brain circuits. This approach opened a new neuroscience of behavior that complemented the prevailing views that psychological factors and early environments dictate who we are.

When seeing patients today, I still often think back to Jaime and Curt. Jaime's story sparked my fascination with FTD and made me to want to know everything about the disease's anatomy, behavior, and genetics. My experiences with Jaime forever changed how I approach diagnosis and encouraged me to integrate a person's strengths as well as their weaknesses into my neurological evaluations. Jaime not only inspired me to study FTD, but she also motivated me to help find treatments for the people who suffer from this condition.

Jaime's husband and caregiver, Curt, was also fascinating and enigmatic. His conscientiousness and profound decency triggered my interest in the caregivers of people with neurological and psychiatric conditions. Despite the many bumps along the road, Curt always displayed compassion for his wife, a testament to his own unique social brain wiring. Time and time again, I see Curt's spirit in other caregivers. They respond to their loved ones with nurturance and empathy. Caregivers cope with new challenges each day and follow a path that can be treacherous, but sometimes healing. They are society's unsung heroes. Our capacity to respond in this way is the essence of what makes our species unique, and uniquely successful.

Since first meeting Jaime, I have seen multiple generations of people in her family. Many have developed FTD because of mutations in the progranulin gene. I have also met people from other families afflicted by mutations in progranulin or other genes that cause FTD. For years, I thought that the cycle of social decay followed by early death in these families would never end. Yet recently, driven in part by funding by an extraordinary family who carries the progranulin mutation, science has moved quickly. There are now exciting new treatments that aim to modify or even eliminate FTD caused by progranulin mutations and other genetic causes. With new technologies, it will soon be possible to edit genes in the brain for people who suffer from FTD and other neurological conditions. Today, there is great hope that new medicines will break the tragic cycle of this condition. The day is coming when there will be a cure for genetic forms of FTD, and this progress would never have been possible without people like Curt and Jaime.

We have made considerable progress in understanding FTD during my career, but at times it has been challenging to convince others of the merits of our work. In particular, my research on creativity was questioned. When I met Markus, I was fascinated by his stunning paintings and wrote a brief report that described how his art blossomed as he developed FTD. The report included one of his pictures, a beautiful red flower with petals detailed in a faded yellow. Although published in a prestigious medical journal, critics of the paper suggested that it was random chance that Markus had become an artist in the setting of FTD. They argued that his new talent did not reflect disease-related changes in his brain. That type of skepticism occurs with many new discoveries.

Dr. Benson was steadfast in his support for my work on art and the brain. Buoyed by his encouragement, I continued to explore the neural underpinnings of visual creativity. Dr. Benson taught me to trust my observations and gave me confidence to believe that there was a link between Markus's new interest in painting and his loss of semantic knowledge. In the years that followed, I met more people with FTD and other individuals with focal brain injuries who also had newfound creativity. These artists strengthened my belief that activity in specific brain circuits underlies creativity. Some scientists continue to question whether creativity that arises in FTD, a relatively rare illness, is relevant for our understanding of creativity more generally. But for me, the artists with FTD elucidate profound truths about who we are and why we create.

When I came to UCSF, my career took an extraordinary turn. I am forever grateful to Stanley Prusiner and Stephen Hauser who recruited me, supported my work, and helped me believe that the diseases that I studied could be treated. The colleagues that I have met at UCSF have been truly transformative, and none has been more important to me than my co-author, Virginia Sturm. The people who joined me in my first decade at UCSF—William Seeley, Aimee Kao, Howie Rosen, Joel Kramer, Rosalie Gearhart, Katherine Rankin, Katherine Possin, Adam Boxer, Michael Geschwind, Jennifer Merrilees, and Maria Luisa Gorno Tempini—have helped me to resolve some of the mysteries of neurodegenerative disorders. Their work is bringing us closer to the day when we can reduce the suffering of people with these conditions. I am proud to say that over the years I have seen the work of four UCSF Nobel Laureates applied to our studies of dementia. Today, new generations of researchers at UCSF and elsewhere are sustaining and advancing our efforts to improve knowledge and clinical care.

I will never forget what Jaime, Curt, Thomas, Susan, Clark, Ellen, Amit, Deepak, Lydia, Ron, Markus, James, Anne, Robert, Sam, Heidi, and all the others taught me about the social brain. I am grateful to have met each of them, and I am a better person for knowing them. Research on FTD continues to reveal the circuits in the social brain that give rise to our common humanity. These are the circuits that we need to understand if we are to address the ongoing stresses facing our species and planet.

—Bruce L. Miller, MD

Acknowledgments

Many people have contributed to the stories and ideas we put forth in this book, but foremost, we want to thank our patients and their families for sharing the details of their lives and for entrusting us with their care. Also, none of our clinical work or research would be possible without the support of the faculty and staff at the UCSF Memory and Aging Center.

As a part of our work at UCSF, we teach the neuroscience of human values to fellows at the Global Brain Health Institute. These inspiring fellows come from various professional backgrounds—from the arts to medicine—and are primarily from low- and middle-income countries. Our sessions with them have helped us to refine many of our ideas regarding human values, many of which we discuss in *Mysteries of the Social Brain*. We are indebted to the fellows and remain in awe of their curiosity, motivation, and accomplishments.

We are especially grateful to Caroline Prioleau, Brittany Morin, and Ashlin Roy for their help in creating the figures in the book. We thank Amanda Moon, of Moon and Company, who advised us on our book proposal and offered important guidance on several initial chapter drafts. We also deeply appreciate those who read our completed manuscript and provided thoughtful critiques, including Anil Vora, Jake Broder, Rosalie Gearhart, Elizabeth Ascher, Cindy Weinstein, and Amanda Akers. Anil Vora and Micah Valero provided instrumental administrative assistance at each stage of preparing this manuscript.

It would not be possible for us to conduct our research without the support of our funders. The National Institute of Health and particularly the National Institute of Aging have supported our research programs over many years. The A.W. and Mary Margaret Clausen family, John Douglas French Alzheimer's Foundation, and Global Brain Health Institute have provided funding for our academic positions at UCSF. We are thankful to UCSF and these other agencies for their continued generosity.

Our families have also offered their enduring support throughout the writing process. Deborah, Hannah, and Elliot Miller (see dedication); Seth, Mason, and Addie Whitehead; and Matthew, Simon, and Emmett Sturm were endlessly patient as we worked through various iterations of the book. We are eternally grateful for their encouragement.

Glossary

Alzheimer's disease A neurodegenerative disorder that primarily disrupts episodic memory but can also affect visuospatial processing, executive functioning, and language.

Amyotrophic lateral sclerosis A neurodegenerative disorder (also known as ALS or Lou Gehrig's disease) characterized by prominent loss of strength and movement. It can be associated with frontotemporal dementia.

Aphasia An acquired loss of speech or language.

Autonomic nervous system Pathways that connect the brain to the body and regulate processes that are critical for survival such as heart rate, blood pressure, breathing, digestion, and sexual function.

Behavioral variant of frontotemporal dementia A subtype of frontotemporal dementia that causes changes in social behavior, empathy, motivation, eating behaviors, compulsions, and executive functioning.

Brainstem An area that connects the spinal cord to the cortex and is critical for consciousness, attention, sleep, breathing, heart rate, blood pressure, emotion, mood, and movement.

Central nervous system Comprised of the brain and spinal cord, the central nervous system is the master regulator of behavior, sensation, and movement.

Cerebral cortex The thick, outer layers of tissue on the surface of the brain that can be divided into the frontal, temporal, parietal, and occipital lobes.

Dementia A condition that causes progressive decline in cognition or behavior and disrupts an individual's day-to-day functioning. Dementia is often caused by a neurodegenerative disorder but can be due to other reasons such as a stroke, tumor, or metabolic deficiency such as a thyroid problem or low vitamin B12.

Dementia with Lewy bodies A neurodegenerative disorder characterized by visual hallucinations, delusions, and prominent changes in movement and sleep.

Emotions Emotions are brief states that guide our thoughts and actions by altering physiology, behavior, and feelings, and physiological responses in predictable ways.

Executive function Cognitive processes that include organization, generation of ideas or actions, inhibition of impulses, and working memory. Executive functions allow people to achieve their goals.

Frontal lobe This region in the most anterior part of the brain (behind the forehead) is responsible for executive functions and complex social behaviors.

Frontotemporal dementia Neurodegenerative disorders characterized by language, speech, or behavioral disturbances.

Hemisphere The brain is made up of two symmetrical halves. The left cerebral hemisphere is attuned to speech, language, mathematical skills, and logical thinking. The right cerebral hemisphere is specialized for visuospatial processing, social behavior, and emotions.

Neural circuit (or network) A group of connected neurons that support specific aspects of cognition, language, emotion, sensation, or movement.

Neurodegenerative disorder Diseases of the brain that appear in mid- to late-life and cause progressive damage to specific neural circuits.

Neuron Unique cells in the brain and peripheral nervous system that allow us to think, move, and feel.

Non-fluent variant of primary progressive aphasia A subtype of frontotemporal dementia that causes prominent difficulty with speech production.

Occipital lobe The most posterior lobes in the cerebral cortex, the occipital lobes are responsible for vision.

Parietal lobe Located above the temporal lobes (and between the frontal and occipital lobes), the parietal lobes are critical for language, mathematics, spatial navigation, body awareness, and many aspects of social behavior.

Primary progressive aphasia A group of neurodegenerative disorders that begin with selective difficulty in speech and/or language.

Semantic variant of primary progressive aphasia A subtype of frontotemporal dementia that causes loss of semantic knowledge.

Sign A finding on a physical or cognitive examination that often indicates the loss of function in a part of the body or brain.

Social brain The networks in the brain that support social behavior. Anchored by the frontal and anterior temporal lobes, the social brain allows us to understand the ideas and feelings of others and to form and maintain relationships.

Stroke A stroke occurs when blood flow to a specific part of the brain is impeded and causes damage to brain tissue.

Symptom A mental or physical experience that a person observes and may be indicative of a specific condition or disease.

Temporal lobe The temporal lobes sit below the frontal and parietal lobes and are responsible for processing verbal, visual, and emotional information.

References

1   Nigst, P. R. *et al.* Early modern human settlement of Europe north of the Alps occurred 43,500 years ago in a cold steppe-type environment. *Proceedings of the National Academy of Sciences* **111**, 14394–14399 (2014).

2   Brothers, L. The social brain: A project for integrating primate behavior and neurophysiology in a new domain. *Concepts Neurosci* **1**, 27–51 (1990).

3   Dunbar, R. I. The social brain hypothesis. *Evolutionary Anthropology: Issues, News, and Reviews: Issues, News, and Reviews* **6**, 178–190 (1998).

4   Semendeferi, K., Lu, A., Schenker, N. & Damásio, H. Humans and great apes share a large frontal cortex. *Nature Neuroscience* **5**, 272–276 (2002).

5   Pollard, K. S. *et al.* Forces shaping the fastest evolving regions in the human genome. *PLoS Genetics* **2**, **e168** (2006).

6   Mellaart, J. *A Neolithic town in Anatolia* (Thames & Hudson, 1967).

7   Rosenberg, M. & Redding, R. W. Hallan Çemi and early village organization in eastern Anatolia. In *Life in Neolithic farming communities: Social organization, identity, and differentiation* (ed Ian Kuijt) 39–62 (Springer, 2000).

8   Tooby, J. & Cosmides, L. Friendship and the banker's paradox: Other pathways to the evolution of adaptations for altruism. In *Proceedings-British academy.* Vol. 88, 119–144 (Oxford University Press Inc., 1996).

9   Wright, K. I. K. Domestication and inequality? Households, corporate groups and food processing tools at Neolithic Çatalhöyük. *Journal of Anthropological Archaeology* **33**, 1–33 (2014).

10 Hodder, I. & Cessford, C. Daily practice and social memory at Çatalhöyük. *American Antiquity* **69**, 17–40 (2004).

11 Tomasello, M., Carpenter, M., Call, J., Behne, T. & Moll, H. Understanding and sharing intentions: The origins of cultural cognition. *Behavioral and Brain Sciences* **28**, 675–691 (2005).

12 Boyd, R. & Richerson, P. J. Culture and the evolution of human cooperation. *Philosophical Transactions of the Royal Society B: Biological Sciences* **364**, 3281–3288 (2009).

13 Morriss-Kay, G. M. The evolution of human artistic creativity. *Journal of Anatomy* **216**, 158–176 (2010).

14 Tattersall, I. Human evolution and cognition. *Theory in Biosciences* **129**, 193–201 (2010).

15 Sinclair, A. Art of the ancients. *Nature* **426**, 774–775 (2003).

16 Hauser, M. D., Chomsky, N. & Fitch, W. T. The faculty of language: What is it, who has it, and how did it evolve? *Science (New York, N.Y.)* **298**, 1569–1579 (2002).

17 Miyagawa, S., Lesure, C. & Nóbrega, V. A. Cross-modality information transfer: A hypothesis about the relationship among prehistoric cave paintings, symbolic thinking, and the emergence of language. *Frontiers in Psychology* **9**, 115 (2018).

18 Galaburda, A. M., LeMay, M., Kemper, T. L. & Geschwind, N. Right-left asymmetries in the brain: Structural differences between the hemispheres may underlie cerebral dominance. *Science (New York, N.Y.)* **199**, 852–856 (1978).

19 Azevedo, F. A. *et al.* Equal numbers of neuronal and nonneuronal cells make the human brain an isometrically scaled-up primate brain. *Journal of Comparative Neurology* **513**, 532–541 (2009).

20 Miller, B. L. & Cummings, J. L. *The human frontal lobes: Functions and disorders.* (Guilford Publications, 2017).

21 Diamond, M. C., Krech, D. & Rosenzweig, M. R. The effects of an enriched environment on the histology of the rat cerebral cortex. *Journal of Comparative Neurology* **123**, 111–119 (1964).

22 Meltzoff, A. N. & Moore, M. K. Newborn infants imitate adult facial gestures. *Child Development* **54**, 702–709 (1983).

23 Waters, S. F., West, T. V. & Mendes, W. B. Stress contagion: Physiological covariation between mothers and infants. *Psychological Science* **25**, 934–942 (2014).

24 Giordano, P. C. Relationships in adolescence. *Annual Review of Sociology* **29**, 257–281 (2003).

25 Luanaigh, C. Ó. & Lawlor, B. A. Loneliness and the health of older people. *International Journal of Geriatric Psychiatry: A Journal of the Psychiatry of Late Life and Allied Sciences* **23**, 1213–1221 (2008).

26 Charles, S. T., Reynolds, C. A. & Gatz, M. Age-related differences and change in positive and negative affect over 23 years. *Journal of Personality and Social Psychology* **80**, 136–151 (2001).

27 Fredrickson, B. L. & Levenson, R. W. Positive emotions speed recovery from the cardiovascular sequelae of negative emotions. *Cognition and Emotion* **12**, 191–220 (1998). https://doi.org/10.1080/026999398379718

28 Mather, M. & Carstensen, L. L. Aging and motivated cognition: The positivity effect in attention and memory. *Trends in Cognitive Sciences* **9**, 496–502 (2005). https://doi.org/10.1016/j.tics.2005.08.005

29 Carstensen, L. L. Social and emotional patterns in adulthood: Support for socioemotional selectivity theory. *Psychology and Aging* **7**, 331 (1992).

30 Kapur, N. Paradoxical functional facilitation in brain-behaviour research. A critical review. *Brain* **119(Pt 5)**, 1775–1790 (1996). https://doi.org/10.1093/brain/119.5.1775

31 Eisenberg, N. *et al.* Relation of sympathy and personal distress to prosocial behavior: A multimethod study. *Journal of Personality and Social Psychology* **57**, 55–66 (1989).

32 Nowak, M. A., Page, K. M. & Sigmund, K. Fairness versus reason in the ultimatum game. *Science (New York, N.Y.)* **289**, 1773–1775 (2000).

33 Edenbrow, M., Bleakley, B. H., Darden, S. K., Tyler, C. R., Ramnarine, I. W. & Croft, D. P. The evolution of cooperation: Interacting phenotypes among social partners. *The American Naturalist* **189**, 630–643 (2017).

34 Bartal, I. B.-A., Decety, J. & Mason, P. Empathy and pro-social behavior in rats. *Science (New York, N.Y.)* **334**, 1427–1430 (2011).

35   De Waal, F. B., Leimgruber, K. & Greenberg, A. R. Giving is self-rewarding for monkeys. *Proceedings of the National Academy of Sciences* **105**, 13685–13689 (2008).

36   McAuliffe, K., Blake, P. R., Steinbeis, N. & Warneken, F. The developmental foundations of human fairness. *Nature Human Behaviour* **1**, 0042 (2017).

37   Gabay, A. S., Radua, J., Kempton, M. J. & Mehta, M. A. The Ultimatum Game and the brain: A meta-analysis of neuroimaging studies. *Neuroscience & Biobehavioral Reviews* **47**, 549–558 (2014).

38   Cordaro, D. T., Sun, R., Keltner, D., Kamble, S., Huddar, N. & McNeil, G. Universals and cultural variations in 22 emotional expressions across five cultures. *Emotion* **18**, 75 (2018).

39   Levenson, R. W. The intrapersonal functions of emotion. *Cognition and Emotion* **13**, 481–504 (1999). https://doi.org/10.1080/026999399379159

40   Carver, C. S. & Harmon-Jones, E. Anger is an approach-related affect: Evidence and implications. *Psychological Bulletin* **135**, 183 (2009).

41   Seeley, W. W. *et al.* Frontal paralimbic network atrophy in very mild behavioral variant frontotemporal dementia. *Archives of Neurology* **65**, 249–255 (2008). https://doi.org/10.1001/archneurol.2007.38

42   Eisenberger, N. I., Lieberman, M. D. & Williams, K. D. Does rejection hurt? An fMRI study of social exclusion. *Science (New York, N.Y.)* **302**, 290–292 (2003).

43   Craig, A. D. How do you feel? Interoception: The sense of the physiological condition of the body. *Nature Reviews Neuroscience* **3**, 655–666 (2002). https://doi.org/10.1038/nrn894

44   Sturm, V. E. *et al.* Prosocial deficits in behavioral variant frontotemporal dementia relate to reward network atrophy. *Brain and Behaviour*, e00807 (2017). https://doi.org/10.1002/brb3.807

45   Perry, D. C., Sturm, V. E., Seeley, W. W., Miller, B. L., Kramer, J. H. & Rosen, H. J. Anatomical correlates of reward-seeking behaviours in behavioural variant frontotemporal dementia. *Brain* **137**, 1621–1626 (2014). https://doi.org/10.1093/brain/awu075

46   Morelli, S. A., Lieberman, M. D. & Zaki, J. The emerging study of positive empathy. *Social and Personality Psychology Compass* **9**, 57–68 (2015).

47   Miller, Z. A. *et al.* Cortical developmental abnormalities in logopenic variant primary progressive aphasia with dyslexia. *Brain Communications* **1**, fcz027 (2019).

48   Van Swieten, J. C. & Heutink, P. Mutations in progranulin (GRN) within the spectrum of clinical and pathological phenotypes of frontotemporal dementia. *The Lancet Neurology* **7**, 965–974 (2008).

49   Chugani, H. T., Behen, M. E., Muzik, O., Juhász, C., Nagy, F. & Chugani, D. C. Local brain functional activity following early deprivation: A study of postinstitutionalized Romanian orphans. *Neuroimage* **14**, 1290–1301 (2001).

50   Ferschmann, L., Bos, M. G., Herting, M. M., Mills, K. L. & Tamnes, C. K. Contextualizing adolescent structural brain development: Environmental determinants and mental health outcomes. *Current Opinion in Psychology* **44**, 170–176 (2022).

51   Meaney, M. J. Maternal care, gene expression, and the transmission of individual differences in stress reactivity across generations. *Annual Review of Neuroscience* **24**, 1161–1192 (2001).

52 Wang, Z. Y. *et al.* Isolation disrupts social interactions and destabilizes brain development in bumblebees. *Current Biology* **32**, 2754–2764. e2755 (2022).

53 Decety, J. & Jackson, P. L. The functional architecture of human empathy. *Behavioral and Cognitive Neuroscience Reviews* **3**, 71–100 (2004). https://doi.org/10.1177/1534582304267187

54 Craig, A. Significance of the insula for the evolution of human awareness of feelings from the body. *Annals of the New York Academy of Sciences* **1225**, 72–82 (2011).

55 Singer, T., Seymour, B., O'Doherty, J., Kaube, H., Dolan, R. J. & Frith, C. D. Empathy for pain involves the affective but not sensory components of pain. *Science (New York, N.Y.)* **303**, 1157–1162 (2004). https://doi.org/10.1126/science.1093535

56 Dobson, S. D. Socioecological correlates of facial mobility in nonhuman anthropoids. *American Journal of Physical Anthropology: The Official Publication of the American Association of Physical Anthropologists* **139**, 413–420 (2009). https://doi.org/10.1002/ajpa.21007

57 Kaminski, J., Waller, B. M., Diogo, R., Hartstone-Rose, A. & Burrows, A. M. Evolution of facial muscle anatomy in dogs. *Proceedings of the National Academy of Sciences* **116**, 14677–14681 (2019).

58 Gross, J. J. Emotion regulation: Current status and future prospects. *Psychological Inquiry* **26**, 1–26 (2015). https://doi.org/10.1080/1047840X.2014.940781

59 Matsumoto, D. Cultural similarities and differences in display rules. *Motivation and emotion* **14**, 195–214 (1990).

60 Ekman, P. & Friesen, W. V. Constants across cultures in the face and emotion. *Journal of Personality and Social Psychology* **17**, 124 (1971). https://doi.org/10.1037/h0030377

61 Shiota, M. N., Campos, B. & Keltner, D. The faces of positive emotion: Prototype displays of awe, amusement, and pride. *Annals of the New York Academy of Sciences* **1000**, 296–299 (2003). https://doi.org/10.1196/annals.1280.029

62 Levenson, R. W., Ekman, P. & Friesen, W. V. Voluntary facial action generates emotion-specific autonomic nervous system activity. *Psychophysiology* **27**, 363–384 (1990). https://doi.org/10.1111/j.1469-8986.1990.tb02330.x

63 Werner, K. H. *et al.* Emotional reactivity and emotion recognition in frontotemporal lobar degeneration. *Neurology* **69**, 148–155 (2007). https://doi.org/10.1212/01.wnl.0000265589.32060.d3

64 de Waal, F. B. The antiquity of empathy. *Science (New York, N.Y.)* **336**, 874–876 (2012). https://doi.org/10.1126/science.1220999

65 Batson, C. D., Fultz, J. & Schoenrade, P. A. Distress and empathy: Two qualitatively distinct vicarious emotions with different motivational consequences. *Journal of Personality* **55**, 19–39 (1987).

66 Blair, R. J. R. Responding to the emotions of others: Dissociating forms of empathy through the study of typical and psychiatric populations. *Consciousness and Cognition* **14**, 698–718 (2005).

67 Rankin, K. P. *et al.* Structural anatomy of empathy in neurodegenerative disease. *Brain* **129**, 2945–2956 (2006). https://doi.org/10.1093/brain/awl254

68 Goldstein, R. L. & Rotter, M. The psychiatrist's guide to right and wrong: Judicial standards of wrongfulness since M'Naghten. *The Bulletin of the American Academy of Psychiatry and the Law* **16**, 359–367 (1988).

69   Harlow, J. M. Passage of an iron rod through the head. *The Boston Medical and Surgical Journal (1828–1851)* **39, 0_1** (1848).

70   Damasio, H., Grabowski, T., Frank, R., Galaburda, A. M. & Damasio, A. R. The return of Phineas Gage: Clues about the brain from the skull of a famous patient. *Science (New York, N.Y.)* **264**, 1102–1105 (1994). https://doi.org/10.1126/science.8178168

71   Kringelbach, M. L. The human orbitofrontal cortex: Linking reward to hedonic experience. *Nature Reviews Neuroscience* **6**, 691–702 (2005).

72   Tinbergen, N. *The study of instinct* (Oxford University Press, 1951).

73   Kringelbach, M. L. & Rolls, E. T. The functional neuroanatomy of the human orbitofrontal cortex: Evidence from neuroimaging and neuropsychology. *Progress in Neurobiology* **72**, 341–372 (2004). https://doi.org/10.1016/j.pneurobio.2004.03.006

74   Small, D. M., Zatorre, R. J., Dagher, A., Evans, A. C. & Jones-Gotman, M. Changes in brain activity related to eating chocolate: From pleasure to aversion. *Brain* **124**, 1720–1733 (2001).

75   Critchley, H. D. & Rolls, E. T. Hunger and satiety modify the responses of olfactory and visual neurons in the primate orbitofrontal cortex. *Journal of Neurophysiology* **75**, 1673–1686 (1996).

76   Possin, K. L. *et al.* Rule violation errors are associated with right lateral prefrontal cortex atrophy in neurodegenerative disease. *Journal of the International Neuropsychological Society* **15**, 354–364 (2009).

77   Tangney, J. P. The self-conscious emotions: Shame, guilt, embarrassment, and pride. In *Handbook of cognition and emotion* (eds T. Dalgleish & M. J. Power) 541–568 (John Wiley & Sons, 1999).

78   Keltner, D. & Buswell, B. N. Embarrassment: Its distinct form and appeasement functions. *Psychological Bulletin* **122**, 250–270 (1997). https://doi.org/10.1037/0033-2909.122.3.250

79   Sturm, V. E., Ascher, E. A., Miller, B. L. & Levenson, R. W. Diminished self-conscious emotional responding in frontotemporal lobar degeneration patients. *Emotion* **8**, 861–869 (2008). https://doi.org/10.1037/a0013765

80   Sturm, V. E. *et al.* Role of right pregenual anterior cingulate cortex in self-conscious emotional reactivity. *Social Cognitive and Affect Neuroscience* **8**, 468–474 (2013). https://doi.org/10.1093/scan/nss023

81   Liljegren, M. *et al.* Criminal behavior in frontotemporal dementia and Alzheimer disease. *JAMA Neurology* **72**, 295–300 (2015). https://doi.org/10.1001/jamaneurol.2014.3781

82   Reid-Proctor, G. M., Galin, K. & Cummings, M. A. Evaluation of legal competency in patients with frontal lobe injury. *Brain Injury* **15**, 377–386 (2001).

83   Markus, H. & Nurius, P. Possible selves. *American Psychologist* **41**, 954 (1986).

84   Seeley, W. W. & Sturm, V. E. Self-representation and the frontal lobes. In *The human frontal lobes: Functions and disorders* (eds B. L. Miller & J. L. Cummings) 317–334 (The Guilford Press, 2006).

85   Amsterdam, B. Mirror self-image reactions before age two. *Developmental Psychobiology* **5**, 297–305 (1972). https://doi.org/10.1002/dev.420050403

86   Gallup Jr, G. G. & Anderson, J. R. Self-recognition in animals: Where do we stand 50 years later? Lessons from cleaner wrasse and other species. *Psychology*

of Consciousness: Theory, Research, and Practice **7**, **46** (2020). https://doi.org/10.1037/cns0000206

87 Bromberg-Martin, E. S. & Sharot, T. The value of beliefs. *Neuron* **106**, 561–565 (2020). https://doi.org/10.1016/j.neuron.2020.05.001

88 Miller, B. L., Seeley, W. W., Mychack, P., Rosen, H. J., Mena, I. & Boone, K. Neuroanatomy of the self: Evidence from patients with frontotemporal dementia. *Neurology* **57**, 817–821 (2001). https://doi.org/10.1212/wnl.57.5.817

89 Shdo, S. M. *et al.* Enhanced positive emotional reactivity in frontotemporal dementia reflects left-lateralized atrophy in the temporal and frontal lobes. *Cortex* **154**, 405–420 (2022). https://doi.org/10.1016/j.cortex.2022.02.018

90 Robertson, I. *How confidence works: The new science of self-belief* (Random House, 2021).

91 Coltheart, M. The neuropsychology of delusions. *Annals of the New York Academy of Sciences* 1191, 16–26 (2010). https://doi.org/10.1111/j.1749-6632.2010.05496.x

92 Corlett, P. R. *et al.* Prediction error during retrospective revaluation of causal associations in humans: fMRI evidence in favor of an associative model of learning. *Neuron* **44**, 877–888 (2004). https://doi.org/10.1016/j.neuron.2004.11.022

93 Capgras, J. & Reboul-Lachaux, J. L'Illusion des 'sosies' dans un delire systematise chronique. *Bulletin de la Societe Clinique de Medicine Mentale* **11**, 6–16 (1923).

94 Hirstein, W. & Ramachandran, V. S. Capgras syndrome: A novel probe for understanding the neural representation of the identity and familiarity of persons. *Proceedings of the Royal Society of London. Series B: Biological Sciences* **264**, 437–444 (1997). https://doi.org/10.1098/rspb.1997.0062

95 Darby, R. R., Laganiere, S., Pascual-Leone, A., Prasad, S. & Fox, M. D. Finding the imposter: Brain connectivity of lesions causing delusional misidentifications. *Brain* **140**, 497–507 (2017). https://doi.org/10.1093/brain/aww288

96 Gusnard, D. A., Akbudak, E., Shulman, G. L. & Raichle, M. E. Medial prefrontal cortex and self-referential mental activity: Relation to a default mode of brain function. *Proceedings of the National Academy of Sciences* **98**, 4259–4264 (2001). https://doi.org/10.1073/pnas.071043098

97 Renoult, L., Irish, M., Moscovitch, M. & Rugg, M. D. From knowing to remembering: The semantic–episodic distinction. *Trends in Cognitive Sciences* **23**, 1041–1057 (2019). https://doi.org/10.1016/j.tics.2019.09.008

98 Tulving, E. "Episodic and semantic memory," in *Organization of memory* (eds E. Tulving & W. Donaldson), 381 (Academic Press, 1972).

99 Pettigrew, T. F. Generalized intergroup contact effects on prejudice. *Personality and Social Psychology Bulletin* **23**, 173–185 (1997).

100 Weisberg, R. W. *Creativity and knowledge: A challenge to theories.* (Cambridge University Press, 1999).

101 Amabile, T. M. The social psychology of creativity: A componential conceptualization. *Journal of Personality and Social Psychology* **45**, 357 (1983).

102 Baltes, P. B. & Staudinger, U. M. Wisdom: A metaheuristic (pragmatic) to orchestrate mind and virtue toward excellence. *American Psychologist* **55**, 122 (2000).

103 Frensch, P. A. & Sternberg, R. J. Expertise and intelligent thinking: When is it worse to know better?. In *Advances in the psychology of human intelligence* 157–188 (Psychology Press, 2014).

104 Sacks, O. *The man who mistook his wife for a hat.* (Simon & Schuster, 1970).

105   Hubbard, E. M. & Ramachandran, V. S. Neurocognitive mechanisms of synesthesia. *Neuron* **48**, 509–520 (2005).
106   Benson, D. F. Language in the left hemisphere. In *The dual brain: Hemispheric specialization in humans* (eds D. F. Benson & E. Zaidel) 193–203. (The Guilford Press, 1985).
107   Wernicke, C. *Der aphasische symptomencomplex.* (Breslau, 1874).
108   Mesulam, M. M. Primary progressive aphasia. *Annals of Neurology* **49**, 425–432 (2001).
109   Geschwind, N. Language and the brain. *Scientific American* **226**, 76–83 (1972).
110   Gorno-Tempini, M. L. *et al.* Classification of primary progressive aphasia and its variants. *Neurology* **76**, 1006–1014 (2011).
111   Hodges, J. R., Graham, N. & Patterson, K. Charting the progression in semantic dementia: Implications for the organisation of semantic memory. *Memory* **3**, 463–495 (1995).
112   Guo, C. C. *et al.* Anterior temporal lobe degeneration produces widespread network-driven dysfunction. *Brain* **136**, 2979–2991 (2013). https://doi.org/10.1093/brain/awt222
113   Snowden, J. S., Thompson, J. C. & Neary, D. Famous people knowledge and the right and left temporal lobes. *Behavioural Neurology* **25**, 35–44 (2012).
114   Viskontas, I. V. *et al.* Visual search patterns in semantic dementia show paradoxical facilitation of binding processes. *Neuropsychologia* **49**, 468–478 (2011).
115   Márquez, G. G. One hundred years of solitude. In *Medicine and Literature, Volume Two* 255–272 (CRC Press, 2018).
116   Sternberg, R. J. Implicit theories of intelligence, creativity, and wisdom. *Journal of Personality and Social Osycology* **49**, 607 (1985).
117   Csikszentmihalyi, M. Motivation and creativity: Toward a synthesis of structural and energistic approaches to cognition. *New Ideas in Psychology* **6**, 159–176 (1988).
118   Guilford, J. Creativity research: Past, present and future-the 1950 presidential address to the American Psychological Association. *Frontiers of Creativity Research: Beyond the Basics.* (Bearly Limited, 1950).
119   Broca, P. Remarks on the seat of the faculty of articulated language, following an observation of aphemia (loss of speech). *Bulletin de la Société Anatomique* **6**, 330–357 (1861).
120   Miller, B. L., Ponton, M., Benson, D. F., Cummings, J. & Mena, I. Enhanced artistic creativity with temporal lobe degeneration. *The Lancet* **348**, 1744–1745 (1996).
121   Selfe, L. Nadia: A case of extraordinary drawing ability in an autistic child. In *The child's representation of the world* 31–48 (Springer, 1977).
122   Treffert, D. A. The savant syndrome: an extraordinary condition. A synopsis: Past, present, future. *Philosophical Transactions of the Royal Society B: Biological Sciences* **364**, 1351–1357 (2009).
123   Sacks, O. *An anthropologist on Mars: Seven paradoxical tales* (Vintage, 2012).
124   Sturm, V. E. *et al.* Enhanced visceromotor emotional reactivity in dyslexia and its relation to salience network connectivity. *Cortex* **134**, 278–295 (2021).
125   Seeley, W. W., Crawford, R. K., Zhou, J., Miller, B. L. & Greicius, M. D. Neurodegenerative diseases target large-scale human brain networks. *Neuron* **62**, 42–52 (2009). https://doi.org/10.1016/j.neuron.2009.03.024

126 Zhou, J. *et al.* Divergent network connectivity changes in behavioural variant frontotemporal dementia and Alzheimer's disease. *Brain* **133**, 1352–1367 (2010). https://doi.org/10.1093/brain/awq075

127 Sturm, V. E., Yokoyama, J. S., Seeley, W. W., Kramer, J. H., Miller, B. L. & Rankin, K. P. Heightened emotional contagion in mild cognitive impairment and Alzheimer's disease is associated with temporal lobe degeneration. *Proceedings of the National Academy of Sciences of the United States of America* **110**, 9944–9949 (2013). https://doi.org/10.1073/pnas.1301119110

128 Chow, T. E. *et al.* Increasing empathic concern relates to salience network hyperconnectivity in cognitively healthy older adults with elevated amyloid-β burden. *NeuroImage: Clinical* **37**, **103282** (2023).

129 Seeley, W. W. *et al.* Unravelling Boléro: Progressive aphasia, transmodal creativity and the right posterior neocortex. *Brain* **131**, 39–49 (2008).

130 Friedberg, A. *et al.* Prevalence, timing, and network localization of emergent visual creativity in frontotemporal dementia. *JAMA Neurology* **80**, 377–387 (2023).

131 Powell, J. A. & Menendian, S. The problem of othering: Towards inclusiveness and belonging. *Othering & Belonging* **1**, 14–40 (2016).

132 Baumeister, R. F. & Leary, M. R. The need to belong: Desire for interpersonal attachments as a fundamental human motivation. *Psychological Bulletin* **117**, 497–529 (1995). https://doi.org/10.1037/0033-2909.117.3.497

133 Granovetter, M. S. The strength of weak ties. *American Journal of Sociology* **78**, 1360–1380 (1973).

134 Allen, K.-A. *The psychology of belonging* (Routledge, 2020).

135 Goodenow, C. & Grady, K. E. The relationship of school belonging and friends' values to academic motivation among urban adolescent students. *The Journal of Experimental Education* **62**, 60–71 (1993). https://doi.org/10.1080/00220973.19 93.9943831

136 Cramm, J. M. & Nieboer, A. P. Social cohesion and belonging predict the well-being of community-dwelling older people. *BMC Geriatrics* **15**, 1–10 (2015). https://doi.org/10.1186/s12877-015-0027-y

137 Holt-Lunstad, J., Smith, T. B., Baker, M., Harris, T. & Stephenson, D. Loneliness and social isolation as risk factors for mortality: A meta-analytic review. *Perspectives on Psychological Science* **10**, 227–237 (2015). https://doi.org/10.1177/ 1745691614568352

138 Hawkley, L. C. & Capitanio, J. P. Perceived social isolation, evolutionary fitness and health outcomes: A lifespan approach. *Philosophical Transactions of the Royal Society B: Biological Sciences* **370**, **20140114** (2015). https://doi. org/10.1177/1745691614568352

139 Cacioppo, J. T. *et al.* Loneliness within a nomological net: An evolutionary perspective. *Journal of Research in Personality* **40**, 1054–1085 (2006). https://doi. org/10.1016/j.jrp.2005.11.007

140 Collins, N. L. & Miller, L. C. Self-disclosure and liking: A meta-analytic review. *Psychological Bulletin* **116**, 457 (1994). https://doi.org/10.1037/0033-2909.116.3.457

141 Clark, M. S. & Reis, H. T. Interpersonal processes in close relationships. *Annual Review of Psychology* **39**, 609–672 (1988). https://doi.org/10.1146/annurev. ps.39.020188.003141

142 Jayawickreme, E., Forgeard, M. J. & Seligman, M. E. The engine of well-being. *Review of General Psychology* **16**, 327–342 (2012). https://doi.org/10.1037/ a0027990

143   Fredrickson, B. L., Mancuso, R. A., Branigan, C. & Tugade, M. M. The undoing effect of positive emotions. *Motivation and Emotion* **24**, 237–258 (2000). https://doi.org/10.1023/a:1010796329158

144   Fredrickson, B. L. The broaden-and-build theory of positive emotions. *Philosophical Transactions of the Royal Society of London Series B Biological Series* **359**, 1367–1378 (2004). https://doi.org/10.1098/rstb.2004.1512

145   Lyubomirsky, S., King, L. & Diener, E. The benefits of frequent positive affect: Does happiness lead to success? *Psychological Bulletin* **131**, 803 (2005). https://doi.org/10.1037/0033-2909.131.6.803

146   Diener, E. & Seligman, M. E. Beyond money: Toward an economy of well-being. *Psychological Science in the Public Interest* **5**, 1–31 (2004). https://doi.org/10.1111/j.0963-7214.2004.00501001.x

147   Sturm, V. E. *et al.* Prosocial deficits in behavioral variant frontotemporal dementia relate to reward network atrophy. *Brain and Behavior* **7**, **e00807** (2017). https://doi.org/10.1002/brb3.807

148   Curry, O. S., Rowland, L. A., Van Lissa, C. J., Zlotowitz, S., McAlaney, J. & Whitehouse, H. Happy to help? A systematic review and meta-analysis of the effects of performing acts of kindness on the well-being of the actor. *Journal of Experimental Social Psychology* **76**, 320–329 (2018). https://doi.org/10.1016/j.jesp.2018.02.014

149   McKnight, P. E. & Kashdan, T. B. Purpose in life as a system that creates and sustains health and well-being: An integrative, testable theory. *Review of General Psychology* **13**, 242–251 (2009). https://doi.org/10.1037/a0017152

150   Ryff, C. D. Happiness is everything, or is it? Explorations on the meaning of psychological well-being. *Journal of Personality and Social Psychology* **57**, **1069** (1989). https://doi.org/10.1037/0022-3514.57.6.1069

151   Windsor, T. D., Curtis, R. G. & Luszcz, M. A. Sense of purpose as a psychological resource for aging well. *Developmental Psychology* **51**, 975 (2015). https://doi.org/10.1037/dev0000023

152   McGregor, I. & Little, B. R. Personal projects, happiness, and meaning: On doing well and being yourself. *Journal of Personality and Social Psychology* **74**, 494 (1998). https://doi.org/10.1037/0022-3514.74.2.494

153   Baumeister, R. F., Vohs, K. D., Aaker, J. L. & Garbinsky, E. N. Some key differences between a happy life and a meaningful life. *The Journal of Positive Psychology* **8**, 505–516 (2013). https://doi.org/10.1080/17439760.2013.830764

154   Lambert, N. M., Stillman, T. F., Baumeister, R. F., Fincham, F. D., Hicks, J. A. & Graham, S. M. Family as a salient source of meaning in young adulthood. *The Journal of Positive Psychology* **5**, 367–376 (2010). https://doi.org/10.1080/17439760.2010.516616

155   Anderson, N. D. *et al.* The benefits associated with volunteering among seniors: A critical review and recommendations for future research. *Psychological Bulletin* **140**, 1505 (2014). https://doi.org/10.1037/a0037610

156   Hill, P. L., Sin, N. L., Turiano, N. A., Burrow, A. L. & Almeida, D. M. Sense of purpose moderates the associations between daily stressors and daily well-being. *Annals of Behavioral Medicine* **52**, 724–729 (2018). https://doi.org/10.1093/abm/kax039

157 Goetz, J. L., Keltner, D. & Simon-Thomas, E. Compassion: An evolutionary analysis and empirical review. *Psychological Bulletin* **136**, 351–374 (2010). https://doi.org/10.1037/a0018807

158 Moskowitz, J. T. *et al*. Measuring positive emotion outcomes in positive psychology interventions: A literature review. *Emotion Review* **13**, 60–73 (2021). https://doi.org/10.1177/1754073920950811

159 Keltner, D. & Haidt, J. Approaching awe, a moral, spiritual, and aesthetic emotion. *Cognition and Emotion* **17**, 297–314 (2003). https://doi.org/10.1080/02699930302297

160 Chirico, A., Glaveanu, V. P., Cipresso, P., Riva, G. & Gaggioli, A. Awe enhances creative thinking: An experimental study. *Creativity Research Journal* **30**, 123–131 (2018). https://doi.org/10.1080/10400419.2018.1446491

161 Sturm, V. E. *et al*. Big smile, small self: Awe walks promote prosocial positive emotions in older adults. *Emotion* (2020). https://doi.org/10.1037/emo0000876

162 Carman, J. B. & Streng, F. J. *Spoken and unspoken thanks: Some comparative soundings*. Vol. **5** (Harvard University, 1989).

163 Emmons, R. A. & Stern, R. Gratitude as a psychotherapeutic intervention. *Journal of Clinical Psychology* **69**, 846–855 (2013). https://doi.org/10.1002/jclp.22020

164 Bartlett, M. Y. & DeSteno, D. Gratitude and prosocial behavior: Helping when it costs you. *Psychological Science* **17**, 319–325 (2006). https://doi.org/10.1111/j.1467-9280.2006.01705.x

165 Algoe, S. B., Gable, S. L. & Maisel, N. C. It's the little things: Everyday gratitude as a booster shot for romantic relationships. *Personal Relationships* **17**, 217–233 (2010). https://doi.org/10.1111/j.1475-6811.2010.01273.x

166 Algoe, S. B., Haidt, J. & Gable, S. L. Beyond reciprocity: Gratitude and relationships in everyday life. *Emotion* **8**, 425 (2008). https://doi.org/10.1037/1528-3542.8.3.425

167 Algoe, S. B., Dwyer, P. C., Younge, A. & Oveis, C. A new perspective on the social functions of emotions: Gratitude and the witnessing effect. *Journal of Personality and Social Psychology* **119**, **40** (2020). https://doi.org/10.1037/pspi0000202

168 Emmons, R. A. & McCullough, M. E. Counting blessings versus burdens: An experimental investigation of gratitude and subjective well-being in daily life. *Journal of Personality and Social Psychology* **84**, 377–389 (2003). https://doi.org/10.1037/0022-3514.84.2.377

169 Lambert, N. M., Graham, S. M., Fincham, F. D. & Stillman, T. F. A changed perspective: How gratitude can affect sense of coherence through positive reframing. *The Journal of Positive Psychology* **4**, 461–470 (2009). https://doi.org/10.1080/17439760903157182

170 Bonanno, G. A. Loss, trauma, and human resilience: Have we underestimated the human capacity to thrive after extremely aversive events? *American Psychologist* **59**, 20–28 (2004).

171 Collishaw, S., Pickles, A., Messer, J., Rutter, M., Shearer, C. & Maughan, B. Resilience to adult psychopathology following childhood maltreatment: Evidence from a community sample. *Child Abuse & Neglect* **31**, 211–229 (2007). https://doi.org/10.1016/j.chiabu.2007.02.004

172   Southwick, S. M., Bonanno, G. A., Masten, A. S., Panter-Brick, C. & Yehuda, R. Resilience definitions, theory, and challenges: Interdisciplinary perspectives. *European Journal of Psychotraumatology* **5**, 25338 (2014). https://doi.org/10.3402/ejpt.v5.25338

173   Bonanno, G. A. & Burton, C. L. Regulatory flexibility: An individual differences perspective on coping and emotion regulation. *Perspectives on Psychological Science* **8**, 591–612 (2013). https://doi.org/10.1177/1745691613504116

174   Panter-Brick, C. & Leckman, J. F. Editorial commentary: resilience in child development–interconnected pathways to wellbeing Vol. **54** 333–336 (Wiley Online Library, 2013). https://doi.org/10.1111/jcpp.12057

175   Pennebaker, J. W. & Seagal, J. D. Forming a story: The health benefits of narrative. *Journal of Clinical Psychology* **55**, 1243–1254 (1999). https://doi.org/10.1002/(SICI)1097-4679(199910)55:**10<1243::AID-JCL**P6>3.0.CO;2-N

176   Aristotle. *Nicomachean ethics* (Oxford University Press, 1998).

177   Ryff, C. D. & Singer, B. H. Know thyself and become what you are: A eudaimonic approach to psychological well-being. *Journal of Happiness Studies* **9**, 13–39 (2008). https://doi.org/10.1007/s10902-006-9019-0

178   Schlegel, R. J., Hicks, J. A., Arndt, J. & King, L. A. Thine own self: True self-concept accessibility and meaning in life. *Journal of Personality and Social Psychology* **96**, 473 (2009). https://doi.org/10.1037/a0014060

179   Torre, J. B. & Lieberman, M. D. Putting feelings into words: Affect labeling as implicit emotion regulation. *Emotion Review* **10**, 116–124 (2018).

180   Hoemann, K., Nielson, C., Yuen, A., Gurera, J. W., Quigley, K. S. & Barrett, L. F. Expertise in emotion: A scoping review and unifying framework for individual differences in the mental representation of emotional experience. *Psychological Bulletin* **147**, 1159 (2021). https://doi.org/10.1037/bul0000327

181   Lukic, S. *et al.* Higher emotional granularity relates to greater inferior frontal cortex cortical thickness in healthy, older adults. *Cognitive, Affective, & Behavioral Neuroscience* **23**, 1401–1413 (2023). https://doi.org/10.3758/s13415-023-01119-y

182   Gergen, K. J. & Gergen, M. M. Narrative and the self as relationship. In *Advances in experimental social psychology* Vol. **21** 17–56 (Elsevier, 1988).

183   Pennebaker, J. W. Putting stress into words: Health, linguistic, and therapeutic implications. *Behaviour Research and Therapy* **31**, 539–548 (1993). https://doi.org/10.1016/0005-7967(93)90105-4

184   Ericsson, K. A. & Lehmann, A. C. Expert and exceptional performance: Evidence of maximal adaptation to task constraints. *Annual Review of Psychology* **47**, 273–305 (1996). https://doi.org/10.1146/annurev.psych.47.1.273

185   Sternberg, R. J. & Lubart, T. I. Investing in creativity. *American Psychologist* **51**, 677 (1996).

186   St-Louis, A. C. & Vallerand, R. J. A successful creative process: The role of passion and emotions. *Creativity Research Journal* **27**, 175–187 (2015). https://doi.org/10.1080/10400419.2015.1030314

187   Kashdan, T. B., Rose, P. & Fincham, F. D. Curiosity and exploration: Facilitating positive subjective experiences and personal growth opportunities. *Journal of Personality Assessment* **82**, 291–305 (2004). https://doi.org/10.1207/s15327752jpa8203_05

188   Oppezzo, M. & Schwartz, D. L. Give your ideas some legs: The positive effect of walking on creative thinking. *Journal of Experimental Psychology: Learning, Memory, and Cognition* **40**, 1142 (2014). https://doi.org/10.1037/a0036577

189 Lindauer, M. S. The span of creativity among long-lived historical artists. *Creativity Research Journal* **6**, 221–238 (1993). https://doi.org/10.1080/104 00419309534480

190 Gardner, H. & Hatch, T. Educational implications of the theory of multiple intelligences. *Educational Researcher* **18**, 4–10 (1989). https://doi.org/10.3102/ 0013189X018008004

191 Resende, E. d. P. F. *et al.* White matter microstructure in illiterate and low-literate elderly Brazilians: Preliminary findings. *Cognitive and Behavioral Neurology* **31**, 193–200 (2018). https://doi.org/10.1097/WNN.0000000000000173

192 Kidd, D. C. & Castano, E. Reading literary fiction improves theory of mind. *Science (New York, N.Y.)* **342**, 377–380 (2013). https://doi.org/10.1126/science. 1239918

193 McCullough, M. E. Savoring life, past and present: Explaining what hope and gratitude share in common. *Psychological Inquiry* **13**, 302–304 (2002).

Index